A Heritage to Remember

Growing Up Poor But Blessed In A Small Midwestern Town

Orpha Sanders Barnes

authorHOUSE®

AuthorHouse™
1663 Liberty Drive
Bloomington, IN 47403
www.authorhouse.com
Phone: 1-800-839-8640

First published by AuthorHouse   5/5/2011

ISBN: 978-1-4567-5932-2 (sc)
ISBN: 978-1-4567-5933-9 (e)
ISBN: 978-1-4567-5934-6 (dj)

Library of Congress Control Number: 2011907194

Printed in the United States of America

Any people depicted in stock imagery provided by Thinkstock are models, and such images are being used for illustrative purposes only. Certain stock imagery © Thinkstock.

This book is printed on acid-free paper.

Author photo by Gordon O'Brien – O'Brien Images, Rochester Hills, MI

Dedicated to the memory of my parents,
Amos Leslie and Clara Edith Sanders

A Tribute to My Parents

Those days at home were like a book
In which we note each page and look
For turned-down leaves from yesteryears
Which tell of numerous laughs and tears.

Many lessons we learned from Mother and Dad,
But the greatest by far that we ever had
Was the example they set in their lives each day
As they read the Bible and took time to pray.

They lived their faith before us each day,
In an unselfish, loving, and Christ-like way,
They believed God's Word and proved His grace,
Assured that no heartache His love can't erase.

That spiritual heritage has been our gain,
The lessons they taught us still remain,
Though years have passed, they are teaching yet,
Their precepts remembered; how could we forget?

Introduction

Quite a few years ago, when I was working in Phoenix, I had my lunch hour alone, so I started writing about my early years at home. Putting these writings into a rhyming form was a novel way to entertain myself. I don't know how many verses I wrote, but they were eventually put aside.

I have moved many times since then. Last summer, I discovered the box containing the original verses and decided I should finish the project.

Much has transpired since the first writing began, and the form is not always the same in the later verses.

I have tried to recall the facts based on accounts from my brothers and sisters, as well as other relatives.

Although this has perhaps been my most ambitious writing effort, it has brought me much satisfaction. I hope it will do the same for you.

Orpha Barnes
Rochester, Michigan
January 2011

THROUGH MEMORY'S LENS I keenly gaze
At myriad scenes from childhood days,
And as I pause and reminisce,
My heart beats nods to acquiesce.

I see a small frame house in view
At 345 Sanders Avenue
In it reside nine happy tenants,
Outside Centralia's city limits.

My Mother and Dad were proud to be
Parents of our family tree,
Three sons were theirs to love and train,
And four daughters with unusual names.

Irene, the youngest of the four,
As an infant entered Heaven's door;
Our parents experienced pain and grief,
But through faith in Christ, they found relief.

Mom said of Irene, "She was the prettiest of all,"
With blue eyes and dark hair, she resembled a doll,
Both measles and pneumonia were her affliction,
But God welcomed her with a special benediction.

Aunt Nora explained the death of Irene
To Odessa, using an astronomical scene
She said the little girl was a bright, shining star,
Lighting the heavens up there very far.

This eight-year-old sister was given a clue
To what death brings—a brighter view
Thus her heart understood the reason why
Stars twinkled brightly in the sky.

Each child had his own chores to do,
Cooking, ironing, and cleaning too,
At times, we fussed, fretted, and fumed,
That we must dust furniture and sweep with a broom.

Troy declares that he often grew weary
Of seeing his sisters with eyes all teary,
Arguing who had last washed the dishes,
So he did the job, like a Miss or a Mrs.

That Troy was industrious, I'll have to confess
It was also his duty to clean out the mess
Which the cow had deposited in the red barn.
If you think that was fun, you'd believe any yarn.

Often, Troy was responsible for milking the cow,
While Dad undertook the garden to plow,
With so many growing children to feed,
It was necessary for him both to plant and to weed.

I can almost see Dad now,
Walking straight behind the plow,
Jutting blade down in the soil,
Whistling gaily while he toiled.

In the furrows that were made,
Infant seeds were carefully laid.
He plodded patiently, performing his best,
God, with nature, did the rest.

Raising chickens was part of our enterprise,
We had both the large and the smaller size,
They had to be watered and fed each day,
Inside a fence they were kept at bay.

Usually in the evening, but sometimes in the morn,
We'd gather in our hands some wheat and corn,
Flinging it forthrightly upon the ground,
We soon heard chatters of chicken sound.

With cackles of mirth and great expectation,
The chickens ran to their destination,
Thrusting their beaks down into the soil,
They pecked any other hen trying to foil.

The rooster with his comb all ruby-red,
Strutted and crowed with an uplifted head,
Looking arrogant in his regnant way,
With a sense of importance, he would sway.

To our hens' faithfulness I can attest,
White and brown treasures they laid in their nests,
At times, however, guilty we'd feel,
As eggs from under their warm bodies we'd steal.

One day Dad discovered to his dismay
That someone was smuggling our chickens away,
So a set of wires inside our abode,
To the door of the chicken house he did load.

Late one night shortly thereafter,
We heard loud cackling from the chicken rafter,
Then the electric device, which Dad had manned,
Performed precisely as he had planned.

When the thief opened the chicken house door,
He soon found out what he had in store,
A clanging of bells made him jump the fence,
And we haven't heard of his whereabouts since.

Beside our house ran a railroad track,
Sometimes the trains sped past, sometimes they rolled back,
As the engine whistled, puffing smoke and sparks,
Our dog responded with his shrill barks.

As the train roared by,
Dola and I watched with an inquisitive eye;
We saw people dining (perhaps the wealthier kinds),
And dreams of faraway places filled our minds.

5

Often we counted the boxcars that passed,
Several scores they numbered, from first to last;
Sometimes they jangled as their wheels hit the track,
We waved to the engineer, and he waved back.

To a new brace of pigs did Troy fall heir
Each year; to offer water, feed, and care;
Dad bought them for a rather small fee,
Then asked my brother their caretaker to be.

From several neighbors Troy gathered food,
I think it's called "slop," but that sounds rude,
The pigs put on weight as their bodies grew,
Then Troy, having planned, knew what to do.

When fall arrived, after summer had ceased,
They were sold back to Dad for a price increase;
Troy's earnings were deposited safely in the bank,
His spirits were high, but soon they sank,
For in '33, during the Depression years,
He lost it all; good cause for tears.

When butchering time for a hog arrived,
Dad and a neighbor stood side-by-side,
Wielding their strength and all their might
While the squealing pig fought its last fight.

Soon the aroma of fresh sausage we savored,
While our taste buds with spices were flavored;
Mom's culinary arts pleased us all,
Especially on those cool days in the fall.

While gathering hickory nuts one day,
Scampering just like happy squirrels at play,
We spied some turnips in a nearby lot,
And sampled them freely. We didn't get caught!

Never did we a barber need,
For Dad cut our hair, at his own speed;
We weren't always proud of the finished product,
But he had more money in his pocket.

On cold winter mornings we huddled around
The black coal stove which in the dining room was found,
If too close we approached, the heat burned our nose,
But when we moved away, cold were our toes.

Dad rose first to get the fire started,
That task required someone stouthearted;
He was the shepherd, we the sheep,
His duty the house warm and cozy to keep.

It was his custom to shake the grate,
Then into the ash pan fell the clinkers and slate;
The clinkers were removed and carried out of sight,
Later, he would "bank" the fire at night.

The old outhouse was of our heritage a part,
In winter weather we hurriedly would dart
Out to that cold, unpretentious place
And carry out our transaction with the greatest haste.

We ventured forth in rain and in sleet,
In all kinds of weather—in the sun's blazing heat,
We peered straight ahead, almost breathing a prayer
That no one would notice us walking there.

A catalogue from Sears or Montgomery Ward
Was the only "tissue paper" we could afford;
Its texture could never be compared to Charmin;
Or at least that's the opinion of my brother Norman.

At Halloween time it was rumored around
That several of these buildings uprooted were found;
This was a sad happening for many folk,
And for us, it was no practical joke.

Mother's stature was small,
But large was her spirit;
Her humor was confounding,
If you were caught near it.

On the first day in April she was delighted
With a proper plan on which she'd alighted;
Inside of the pancake batter she made,
A small cloth she'd shrewdly and deviously laid.

As soon as the first bite we displaced,
A sheepish grin appeared on her face,
Her blue eyes sparkled as she spoke,
She told us it was only an April Fool joke.

It was our turn to grin at other times
As she quoted one of her favorite rhymes,
Sounding poetic as she could be
Citing about kitty and the spool of O.N.T.

Picking strawberries made us come alive,
And on May 30, in '35,
Dad and I decided to race;
Of course, we both wanted to win first place.

We crawled along, row after row,
Mashing strawberries as we'd go,
Our red-stained knees, though tough, started aching,
Leg muscles were strained, and our backs were breaking.

Exerting all my strength, I rallied,
One hundred quarts to my credit were tallied,
But Dad was far ahead of me;
(Maybe I hadn't kept an accurate score)
He had a total of nineteen quarts more!

To my brother Troy I'll give due credit,
And this number he did not edit,
His total was a whopping 115;
But our dad remained the "Strawberry King."

Canning fruit was an annual affair,
We peeled bushels of apples, peaches, and pears,
And washed glass jars in suds and hot water,
Squashing foods through a perforated colander.

Mother tightened the lids giving them a twist,
Although she was small, she had power in her wrist;
As perspiration beaded her smiling face,
She labored in our kitchen   her favorite place.

Vegetables were part of the menu she planned,
Hundreds of quarts of these were canned;
Tomatoes, corn, and green beans too,
Were picked fresh from the garden where they grew.

Once Mother made jelly, and on it paraffin poured,
With my finger dipped in it, a small hole I bored,
Chewing the wax, away I ran,
The hole was discovered, and the questions began.

As Norman was known to be a mischievous kid,
He got the scolding while my face I hid;
At camp meeting time I confessed to my mother
I had told a lie while blaming my brother.

The aroma from apple butter coming from the yard,
Was proof that by a kettle Mom was standing guard;
Mixing spices with apples, making a delicious brown spread,
That we put on baked biscuits or homemade bread.

The icebox was a blessing I can't forget;
It had its drawbacks—"Empty the ice pan," and yet,
The milk from our cow and the butter we churned,
Were kept sweet and cold, as we soon learned.

Often used in our kitchen was a crock;
It was almost as needed as the clock;
It held a holiday beverage called "Float,"
That caused us when we saw it to gloat.

When Mom made sauerkraut, it lent
A place for cabbage to ferment;
And headcheese was pressed there to set
Neatly covered with a cloth-like net.

At times, milk was strained into the crock,
And placed to cool in the icebox;
My memories of its usefulness I now unlock,
A boon to us-- that big, brown crock.

Our drinking water was pumped from an outside well;
It was very deep, how far it went I could not tell;
The water from the cistern was used for chores;
Never did we buy water from the stores.

Our rectangular washboard, used to scrub clothes,
Was regarded by some people as one of their woes;
But it readied the clothes for the regular wash,
Loosening stains, stubborn and harsh.

Water was heated on the coal- and wood-burning stove,
Then carried to the back porch to the washing machine;
With Mom's homemade soap and the swishing of suds,
In no time at all the dirty became clean.

After being washed, through the wringer they'd go;
(Today that seems strange, I know);
However, we'd never demoralize our mother,
Because (for her), this was more fun than a free circus show.

The fresh-washed clothes were hung out on a line,
No dryer was ours, but Mom's method was fine,
Because "the sun-dried clothes smell so clean," she'd say,
It was worth her efforts to dry them that way.

Ironing clothes was a duty I'll never forget,
For me it was playing; I have no regret;
I ironed Dad's handkerchiefs one by one,
Thinking of it as being fun.

Our iron had a detachable handle made of wood,
It was less likely to burn and blister as the iron handle could;
'Twas a great innovation I would say,
And we could do our job in a safer way.

While Dola ironed Dad's pants, our oldest sister strove
To smooth out shirt wrinkles with the iron heated on the stove;
Not yet knowing about fabrics of nylon and polyester,
Which would have made the process faster.

While those methods we used for washing, drying, and ironing clothes,
Were much different from those used today,
We never considered for one minute
We were performing those jobs in a crude way.

New inventions today make chores go fast,
But they can't bring happiness that will last,
Our focus should be on appreciating each other,
And treating our neighbor as our brother.

Odessa, Dola, and I slept in the same bed;
I don't remember for how long,
Often Dad came into our room
Singing a traditional song.

Good morning, merry sunshine,
How did you wake so soon?
You've scared the little stars away,
And shined away the moon;
I saw you go to sleep last night

Before I ceased my play;
How did you get way over there,
And, pray, where did you stay?

I never go to sleep, dear child,
I just go 'round to see,
My little children of the East,
Who rise and watch for me;
I waken all the birds and bees,
And flowers on my way,
And now come back to see the child,
Who stayed out late at play.

Later, I thought: What a pleasant way
To wake up for the day
Hearing a song from Dad,
To show he was happy, not sad.

In those early years, Dola and I earned a small income
With our dad's assistance; he met us after school
In our backyard, as a general rule,
Where he had cleaned some bunches of onions and radishes,
That we took to peoples' door,
Hoping to make a sale of five cents a bunch (no more).

Dola was thirteen, and I was eleven,
And we didn't get home until after seven,
With only fifty-five cents as the total sum,
Barely enough to buy a few packages of gum;
But we understood that we could only keep what we'd earned;
It was an important lesson for us to have learned.

Another project of which we were part,
And was close to our church members' hearts,
Was raising funds for the Woodstock Children's Home;
And as a means of motivation,
A prize was given to the one with the highest donation.

Dola and I entreated many to give,
To help those children
Whose circumstances caused them to live
Without a father or mother
And perhaps no sister or brother.

After a few months, we took our little blue bank
To the church; our solicitors to thank;
When the winner was announced (I think on a Sunday),
I was surprised I'd collected the most money.

I received an *Egermeier's Bible Story Book*,
Along with a beautiful blue fountain pen,
As well as a plaque of the Ten Commandments;
But I was most excited to know
That those children had reaped what I sowed.

⁓✥⁓

Norman was a sports enthusiast,
And the sport I loved watching him do,
Was pole-vaulting in the field in front of our house;
And I must admit, I tried it too.

With his hands on the pole and the crossbar in sight,
Hoping to clear, he'd sprint with all his might;
As each height was reached, the bar he'd raise,
While excitedly we'd cheer, and offer our praise.

No other neighbor was as skilled
As Norman, our brother.
When comparisons were attempted
There was no other.

Norman also was adept at broad jumping;
(How could I forget?)
At 11 feet, 4 and ¾ inches
A new record was set;
He was not quite ten (It was '36);

Yet, at that early age, he knew all the tricks.

At the annual Sub-Urban Track and Field meet,
Athletes gathered to compete,
Many congratulations that day were spoken,
When fifteen past records were broken.

One of these was in the 200-yard relay,
Which included Norman, Arthur Ballantini,
Charles Stone, and Hubert Gherardini;
This distance was run in 32 seconds;
That seems pretty fast, but how can I say?

In this same meet, four girls from our school
(Including me)
Also set a new record—in our 200-yard relay;
And I know that all of us agree
That our school was outstanding
In more than one way.

Doing push-ups (for Troy) was a great thrill;
His P.E. teacher, after observing the drill,
Used Troy's performance and athletic skill
As an example—"There's always a way
Where there's a will."

I joined my brothers in outdoor fun,
Proudly competing with each one;
Athletic endeavors were part of our life
But never did they cause sibling strife.

One pastime which we greatly enjoyed
Was chinning ourselves;
Our energies we employed
To develop our muscles and make them stronger,
By holding on to the support just a little longer.

With our hands grasping that metal bar,

We'd raise ourselves up just so far
Until our chin with the bar was level;
Then inwardly with joy we'd revel.

For baseball games there was no ration,
For another kind of recreation;
Neighbors joined us in a large, open field,
Our thrill at Dad's homeruns was not concealed.

One of the favorite games we knew,
A popular one, which we never outgrew,
Was that of marbles—those crystallized spheres,
Of which we hold memories after all these years.

Invariably we noted the different hues,
Admiring the reds, yellows, and blues,
Some had an appearance that was mottled,
Others were kept in a container, bottled.

A striped marble, called an agate,
Was sometimes used by our friend, George Daggett,
When he and Norman together would play,
There was much excitement, I dare say,

One or more of the marbles was arranged
Inside a circle; and skill, not age,
Was the prerequisite; (What force was used!)
To give up defeated, they each refused.

With one of the marbles, propelled by the thumb,
They shot toward the circle, hoping to hit some,
Whoever succeeded in knocking them out,
Was known as the winner, without any doubt.

All three boys had a paper route,

Which afforded exercise, but not much loot;
For several miles they rode on their bikes,
Hearing customers cite their likes and dislikes.

Troy was first a carrier to be,
Two cents per customer per week was his fee;
But when Everett carried, some years after that,
The fee had risen to fifteen cents flat.

Generously, Everett took three cents off his pay
Per customer (when there was a holiday);
But *The Sentinel* office was not amused,
To recognize any "docks," they utterly refused.

Many times we kids gathered 'round
To help fold the papers as we sat on the ground;
Then the papers were placed in a gray canvas bag,
Which was loaded so heavily it tended to sag.

Because our brothers had to travel so far,
In inclement weather Dad took them by car;
Their forceful throws caused those Sentinels to soar,
At times, they landed near the recipient's door.

One memorable day (so long ago it seems),
I had an experience like a pleasant dream;
Entering our dining room, I was surprised to hear
An unfamiliar voice with my listening ear.

I walked in the direction from where it came,
Hoping to match the voice with a name;
Instead I beheld with steadfast eyes
Our first radio; a marvelous surprise.

That means of communication—a national toy;

Brought to our family inexpressible joy;
We listened to soap operas, and comedy dandy,
Such as the popular one called Amos 'n' Andy.

That program exemplified many men in those days,
With no money, no job, and little praise;
Dad followed their plights from beginnings to ends,
As though they were his personal friends.

One radio entertainer whom we enjoyed so well
Was a singer of ballads with the name Lulu Belle;
She and Skyland Scotty teamed together for awhile,
Singing and yodeling in unique hillbilly style.

Asher Sizemore, with "Little Jimmy," his son,
Sang sometimes as a duo, other times as only one,
Closing each night's program, their vigil they'd keep,
With "Little Jimmy" singing, "Now I Lay Me Down to Sleep ..."

The program, Lum and Abner,
Aired in their "Jot 'em Down Store,"
Had dialect humor, interspersed with rural lore;
When we wanted something different,
By simply turning the dial,
We could hear music played in classical style.

During World War II, the radio linked
The people at home (with different toil)
With those on the battlefields, on foreign soil;
Several reporters (each one worthwhile),
Delivered the news in a personal style.

One commentator, Gabriel Heater, by name,
(With no thought for personal acclaim),
Instilled optimism for those soldiers in fight,
With his opening phrase, "There's good news tonight."

The action focused on domestic issues;

The Depression persisted; "Could we buy shoes?"
"Who would be elected the next president"?
"Would Roosevelt or Dewey to the White House be sent"?

Another program on the air
(The March of Time)
Made us feel that we were there;
Van Voorhis, the narrator of the day's events,
Reported what had happened with terse comments.

We envisioned the rise of Hitler as he became more aggressive,
We saw a king resign his kingship to claim a love more possessive;
Time marched along, and we stepped into pace
Taking note of world events from every clime and place.

Lowell Thomas is another name I remember,
Faithfully, he reported happenings from January to December,
Although the news was sometimes grim,
These men showed compassion filled to the brim.

⁓✳⁓

Odessa's schooling started earlier than ours,
But at the beginning she had Miss Bowers;
The same teacher who taught all of us in grade one;
With her large-lettered cards, she made learning fun.

Mrs. Knappenberger was the instructor in the second grade;
(In those days, teachers weren't well-paid);
And Miss Hahn, in grade three,
Kept them as busy as a worker bee.
Aunt Ollie was her teacher in grade four,
She taught in that school for three decades or more.

Margaret Cantrell who was in that same class,
Wanted Odessa an answer to pass,
But Odessa didn't comply;
For Aunt Ollie was watching with her wise teacher's eye.

Miss Wayman all unruly boys heeded,
Stern discipline was applied when needed;
She kept a large paddle plainly exhibited,
Today, that kind of punishment is prohibited.

A popular song that the kids liked to sing,
Was one that caused their ears to ring:
"Little Orphan Annie's Come to Our House to Stay,"
Then recess time arrived, and they hurried to play.

Living with us while she taught school,
Was Aunt Alma Coates, Uncle Ivan's own jewel;
But he persuaded her to become his wife,
So she traded teaching for a homemaker's life.

Before that decision was ever reached,
She was given the fifth grade to teach;
Odessa was one of her pupils then;
They studied the lives of some famous men.

They learned a poem about Paul Revere,
Of his midnight ride in that well-known year;
"To make memorizing easier," Aunt Alma said,
"The poem in its entirety should be read."

So they read the verses from beginning to end,
Then started over and read them again,
Continuing with this suggested plan,
They memorized most of the poem of that famous man.

Sometimes the school had a special event
To add money to the budget when it had a dent;
The occasion, called a "pie social," was well attended,
But one time a certain fellow was offended.

He bid on a butterscotch pie Odessa brought,
Assuming that she'd eat with him, as she surely ought,
But while he sat and waited, he must have muttered groans,
Because she was so bashful, he was left to eat alone.

We walked to school almost every day,
Noticing diversions along the way;
While crossing the bridge, we gleefully yakked,
Off in the distance was the railroad track.

The trees in the orchard through which we trampled,
Held luscious pears, which we eagerly sampled;
While we looked for more, our mouths would drool,
Then across the road we beheld our school.

Aunt Ollie, the principal, rang the school bell,
What time it was we couldn't tell,
Nevertheless, we hurried fast
To line up in rows in front of our class.

Our teachers were some of the very best,
Their daily lesson plans were packed with zest,
Their methods of teaching were first-rate,
At inspiring confidence they were great.

Iva Bowers was the first to plant the seed
Of our formal education; She taught us to read;
Her patience and kindness were beyond measure,
Her pupils were her greatest treasure.

My third and fourth grade teacher was one
Who believed that learning should be lots of fun,
She offered a prize to the pupil in turn
Who was the first the states and capitals to learn.

I was determined to win that award,
Studying diligently of my own accord,
I worked that night for several hours,
Using all my memorizing and spelling powers.

The next day at school I was happy to relate,
"I know every one of the capitals and states."
But Ruth Marlow looked at me rather aghast,
She wondered how I'd completed that task so fast.

I could tell that she was very surprised,
When I saw the questioning look in her eyes,
But I wrote them all, missing only one,
She reconsidered and said that I'd won.

For the gift I earned, I was extremely glad;
Hurrying home, I showed it to Mother and Dad,
There were pencils, crayons, and a compass, all new
In a box with drawers—a pleasing view.

Blanche Stoafer was my teacher in the fifth and sixth grade;
Some effective study habits by her were laid,
As a disciplinarian, she was one of the best,
She got good results; I'll have to confess.

While she worked with the fifth graders one day,
We in the sixth grade decided to play,
Instead of the Greek gods and goddesses learning,
For laughter and conversation we were yearning.

In an instant, she turned toward us her face,
Informing us, "This is a disgrace,
Those gods and goddesses whom you consider fables,
Are as important to learn as your times tables."

In poetic form she wrote a traffic safety song,
Which I have remembered these many years long;
Her effervescent spirit, and her attractive face,
From my memory I can never erase.

Aunt Ollie, the principal of our school,
Knew how to administer learning's tool,
To help us bring about a successful completion
To our first eight grades' education.

She helped us solve problems of percent,
While vast amounts of time she lent,
Staying after school for many hours
Testing Dola's and my spelling powers.

Many Italians came to our school,
We soon discovered that a usual rule
Applied to the spelling of their surname;
The last letter in it was often the same.

Edna Mae Castellari is one I know;
Let me see how far I can go,
While Elmer Ballantini, who was in my class,
Won first place in a 50-yard dash.

Knute Castellari, the oldest and tallest boy in school,
Asked Miss Stoafer for a date, which was simply not kosher;
And when she refused, no doubt he felt spurned,
But that was an important lesson he learned.

Geno Gallasini liked his teacher, Aunt Ollie,
He lived near Aunt Ruth and Uncle Rollie;
And about Guy Bernabi, I'll tell you later;
He was a dear friend, our next-door neighbor.

Evio Pollaci everyone knew,
He must have worn a size twelve shoe;
Why he was called "Preach," I do not know,
But I remember that it was so.

About Norma Donini—what shall I say?
She and I ran a 200-yard relay;
The East Wamac girls won first place,
In the Sub-Urban Track & Field race.

As I have shown, these names end the same;
They are examples; it's not just a game;
One name however ended in an "O,"
It's a positive fact that Norman knows
Whose it was; he'll tell you so;
A fighter, Marie Chiavarrio.

I'll never forget that February when
My birthday arrived, and I became ten;
My scheming mother in anticipation,
Planned for me a great celebration.

Without my knowing it, she had confided
In my teachers at school; they were invited
To come to our house for a noon-time meal,
Promising the secret not to spill.

That birthday dinner was so delicious,
And to think that I didn't have to wash dishes;
The cake Mom baked was the very best;
How glad I was to be the honored guest!

Mother and Dad an agreement made,
That Rawleigh Products they would trade
To Naomi Westerfeld if she'd consent to be
Our piano teacher, for no further fee.

Playing diligently and timed by the clock,
We had selections by Beethoven and Bach;
Our aspiring teacher hoped to impart
A love of great music right from the start.

The younger children Odessa did teach,
A time to practice was assigned to each;
Troy's schedule—hats off to him!
For several months was at 5:00 am.

I agree that was a relentless hour,
Yet he played with patience and plenty of power
"Galloping Horses," a recital number,
Waking us from peaceful slumber.

Piano practice wasn't always easy,

For chords and runs left us feeling queasy;
We tried our best those scales to master,
As we played slowly, then much faster.

It was difficult for Norman to sit still,
When sports of all kinds gave him a thrill,
How could he practice with zeal and zest,
When athletically he was so blest?

As for Everett, he didn't watch the clock,
While playing from Schubert or Dvorak,
So it came as no surprise when he was asked to play
For the program on his eighth-grade graduation day.

Schubert's "Ballet Music from Rosamunde"
Was the number Dola and I played
In a recital given by Miss Westerfeld
At the church where the program was held.

In this same church about eight years later
In an organ-and-piano recital presented by Augusta Warskow
Everett and Charles Heaton, his high school friend,
Played several selections, and a favorite, "Finlandia,"
Was played at the very end.

That children's book from which we played,
Is noticeably dated, torn, and frayed,
Numerous stars on the pages are found,
And commendations from our teacher abound.

Our piano was the hub where we often converged,
Blending voices and spirits which together surged,
A happy family with laughter and song,
Joined by Mother and Dad singing along.

One year a certain Streptococcus

In our family caused quite a ruckus;
We were placed in enforced isolation,
Altering our lifestyle's situation.

That disease, which was called scarlet fever,
Kept Mother working like a beaver,
Caring for patients, Troy and me,
While being concerned for the rest of the family.

Dad set up a tent in the front yard,
For the other family members who from us were barred;
If they entered the house they could be given a fine,
For on it was posted a quarantine sign.

While the scarlet fever lingered on,
Troy memorized the first five chapters of John,
He quoted each one, verse by verse,
To me and Mother, our efficient nurse.

I didn't feel ill (well, maybe a speck),
But Troy complained of pains in his neck;
Later, our house was fumigated,
A process which I'm told is now outdated.

Several years later, that disease Dola incurred,
Not realizing the consequences, she did a thing quite absurd,
In order to keep those scholarly A's stacked,
She studied too long and had a setback.

As a result of that illness, her heart was affected;
An irregular beat the doctor detected;
Then the following year, after some months had passed,
She was named valedictorian of her high school class.

Sometimes a pig through the fence would break,

And from the pig pen his exit he'd take,
It usually happened when Dad was away
At camp meeting, or conference, as a delegate lay.

So Mother would walk up and down the alley,
Scanning neighbors' yards, marking her tally,
And then she spotted him, to her dismay
In a friend's garden, a few yards away.

"Here piggy, here piggy," came her call,
With fast-running pace, she took heed not to fall,
Flinging arms high over her head,
She chased him until she was almost dead.

Swerving here and snorting there, the pig arrived at last
To the lodging which he left—not all first-class;
And the hole in the fence was repaired 'ere long,
With apologies offered for the animal's wrong.

At another time when Dad was away,
Mother decided, without further delay,
To renovate a couple of rooms,
These much-used places she would groom.

Using sandpaper, a paintbrush, and varnish too,
With an industrious spirit, but a very small crew,
She finished the dining room—"Phase Number One,"
Proud of the woodwork, pleased it was done.

Next, she moved the kitchen chairs and table
To the dining room, so she would be able
The kitchen floor to clean and paint,
By today's standards, that might seem quaint.

While the kitchen was getting a new look,

In the dining room we would have to cook,
So the kerosene burner, our summer stove,
Was moved also, to our cozy cove.

Now you can be sure that it was crowded there,
With hardly an extra inch to spare,
In our dining room/kitchen combination,
We almost had ourselves to ration.

One Sunday afternoon we traveled by car
To visit the Daggett family—not very far,
We had so much fun; we laughed and clowned,
And finally it was time to be homeward bound.

Approaching the house we were completely dazed,
For our eyes beheld not only a haze,
But sinister smoke (we'd not seen such before),
Rolling out from the windows, as well as the front door.

I jumped from the car—a foolish feat,
Thinking that the auto I could beat,
I would run fast, I reasoned (what fast transportation!),
And rescue my doll from the fire's devastation.

Now Dad, in the meantime, had returned
From church conference; he quickly learned
That the house was locked with no one there,
While smoke surrounded it everywhere.

"Fire!" he shouted, breaking into the place,
Then men from the neighborhood joined in the race,
Carrying furnishings from each smoky room
Saving what they could from gravest doom.

Helplessly, we each stood by,
Feeling sad at heart, and wanting to cry,
Viewing our furniture as it sat in the yard,
Realizing that from our house we were barred.

While I was pondering this complaint,
Someone approached me—an unknown saint;
I don't know whether he was short or tall,
I simply remember that he handed me my doll.

"How did it happen? Where did it start?"
Such wonderment ran rampant in each heart;
After such questions had been posed,
The cause of the fire was disclosed.

Each of us was responsible: we simply forgot
To turn off the burner; so the fire caught
The kettle's wooden handle, 'twas black with char,
And the tablecloth, on the table, loomed near, not far!

The fire extended, spreading from the latter,
To a large ham, contained on a platter,
And the varnished woodwork, with its once-lustrous shine,
Was covered with blisters in the room where we dined.

Mom's work was for naught, yet her spirits revived,
Our house was still standing and we were alive;
And that kerosene stove where the teakettle sat
Is a family tradition we shall never forget.

Early in our lives we learned to pray
In our own simple, child-like way,
And no critical comment to me was made,
When "God bless the Rawleigh man" I prayed.

In the morning or evening of every day
Our family knelt together to pray,
And now, though we'd travel from ocean to ocean,
We could never forget those family devotions.

It was not unusual for us to see,

Dad by his bed, on bended knee,
And to hear him voice our names to God,
Imploring His guidance wherever we'd trod.

Often we heard him pray,
That we might live in such a way,
That sudden death to us would bring,
Instant glory with Christ, our King.

We were encouraged Bible verses to learn;
Each of us joined in, taking our turn
Listening, as verses were repeated,
Noting mistakes and words deleted.

If six verses of scripture we memorized,
Before we could acquire our sought-after prize,
We had to prove that we wouldn't make
More than a maximum of three mistakes.

A Child's Certificate then we'd earn;
But if that kind our pride did spurn,
We could memorize five verses more,
And a Young People's Certificate we could lay in store.

But if a dozen verses we chose to learn,
An Adult Certificate was ours in return;
Wherever we chose to stop or start,
We were learning God's Word by heart.

One year for a Christmas program part,
Mother spoke eloquently from her heart,
Our faces beamed as we sat in our pew,
As she recited Matthew, chapter two.

To Cowden we went to attend our church camp,

With gas stove, food, and a kerosene lamp,
We ate outside with the sky overhead.
At night, we slept on a cot as our bed.

Mother cooked food that was delicious,
We carried water from a well to wash dishes;
The thunder and lightning were at times very frightful,
But those days at camp were so delightful.

Under a tabernacle all of us met,
Songs were sung by an outstanding quartet;
Odessa liked one singer more than the rest,
If you'd ask her his name, she'd say "Virgil Bess."

Scores of children gathered around
On that central Illinois campground;
From Harold Constant we learned many a song,
Which in our memories will linger long.

A vital part of our lives was the church,
Thus, we had little time to search
For ventures with other leadings,
For we were so often at meetings.

The morning worship hour followed Sunday school,
With all of us attending as a general rule;
And again, that evening, under the same steeple,
A service was conducted by the young people.

Topics by a leader were individually assigned
To those who were willing and so inclined;
A limit of time to each speaker was given,
With themes that ranged from "earth" to "heaven."

On such Sunday afternoons we found a nook
Where we researched in magazine and book,
To find ideas for our speech,
So an attentive audience we could reach.

Thus, we learned early before a group to speak,
Even though we trembled and our knees grew weak,
Such experiences of these kinds
Helped to discipline our bodies and minds.

On each Sunday night following the youth hour,
Was preaching of Christ's saving power,
And later on, in the middle of the week,
Came prayer and Bible study—His guidance to seek.

At times, a course was taught by our pastor
On Biblical subjects; He was a master
At teaching the three journeys of St. Paul,
He made the classes interesting for all.

Mother, Dad, and Troy, I'm told
In several of these classes were enrolled;
Faithfully, they attended quite a few nights,
Gaining many spiritual insights.

Afterward, they passed a written test,
They were pleased that they had been so blest;
A certificate was given, a token treasure,
Of inspiration that knew no measure.

I received additional Biblical education;
At fourteen, I completed a course in
"How the Bible Came to Be";
Instructor, Reverend R. L. Thorpe, signed the card
And with a smile congratulated me.

Dad taught a Sunday school class of men,
He loved them as though they were his kin;
Reading avidly from week to week,
Information from various books he'd seek.

Arnold's Commentary was a leading source,
And *Haley's Dictionary* was consulted, of course,
The Bible Atlas and *Strong's Concordance* I know,
Enabled him with Biblical knowledge to grow.

George Bush, a respected member of his class,
Was killed in a horrendous mining blast;
The following Sunday, when roll time came,
Dad wrote "promoted" after Bush's name.

A Sunday school class Mother sometimes had;
But not for as many years as Dad,
Object lessons she sometimes prepared;
She showed those children that she really cared.

In 1938, much excitement did abound
When oil was discovered in our hometown;
Many workers with their families made our population boom,
When they came from other states in search of house and room.

One man who came was Mr. Finger
(What a strange name, I thought),
A job in the oil field he sought;
He moved ahead of his family, I well remember,
For daughter Anita finished school in December.

He lived at first in the church parsonage basement,
Perhaps this was for a reason divinely sent;
For on Mr. Finger's first visit to our church,
Morris Smith asked him to teach a class of boys,
Hoping he could quell any unruly noise.

Mr. Finger was a likeable man, generous in many ways,
Always eager to offer encouragement and praise;
For five years he was superintendent of the Sunday school,
And the attendance increased as a general rule.

Later, the rest of the family came,
Anita, L. Marie, and Lester Howard by name;
Anita and L. Marie stayed in Centralia that year;
When Anita moved later to Greenville, they surely shed a tear.

Lester was a year older than me;
That he was a bit timid, it was plain to see,
When our school had noon movies (for only one cent),
And as his date he hoped I would give my consent,
He found himself too shy to ask,
And beseeched someone else to do that task.

L. Marie, a cute girl, enjoyed being with Troy;
They laughed a lot and her attractiveness she did employ;
She displayed this charm while Troy was milking Bossy one day,
As it was raining while the cow chewed her hay;
Marie, holding an umbrella high,
Shielded Troy from drops in the sky.

Lester and Norman were zealous sport fans;
Often they were seen with a basketball in hand,
Aiming toward the hoop attached to our shed,
Hoping for a "long shot" or a "free throw" instead.

Another pastime brought them lots of pleasure,
It cost Les only $10, but it was quite a treasure,
Enthroned, he looked just like a lord,
Sitting on the seat of his Model T Ford.

George Daggett usually joined them; "Sunny" he was called;
To watch the three of them take off was cause for loud applause,
For certain tactics were required to get the engine running,
There had to be quick-thinking and split-second timing.

First, the throttle was advanced to full speed,
Next, the hand brake was set, for safety indeed;
Then, a radiator wire was pulled out, just enough,
For a properly primed engine, that could be tough.

Les would grasp the crank handle with an upward jerk,
Folding back his thumb to make sure it would work,
For if the engine kicked back, ('twas a probability),
The thumb could be broken—a possibility.

If Les was fortunate, the motor roared to life,
The car shook with tremors, unremitting and rife,
Les then quickly leaped to cut back the throttle,
There was no time to dawdle.

Once in the seat, he'd release the hand brake,
Feeling less vibration, not so many shakes;
Pushing the gearshift pedal down to the floorboard,
With a screeching and shuddering, in low gear they roared.

After some speed was reached—how much I do not know,
The pedal was released as far as it would go;
With the engine shifted thus, from low to high gear,
The Model T was off amid laughs and sometimes a jeer.

They traveled around Centralia on a Sunday afternoon,
Tooting the horns with their two-tone tune;
The price of those horns was deemed to be over par,
For they cost $5 more than Les paid for the car.

After trekking to the lake known as the Reservoir,
They'd return with more trouble with that '23 Model T car;
The fault wasn't with the engine or with a burned-out wire,
But it was what they imagined—another flat tire!

Our neighbors were the friendliest kind,
That ours was a large family, they didn't mind;
Next door to us, Benvenuti by name,
Lived a family who from Italy came;
They were generous people, never rude,
And Norman relished their Italian food.

This proved to be an embarrassing action
For Mother and Dad, this habitual transaction;
The dish ravioli was Norman's joy;
When he came home later, Mom readily surmised
That already he'd eaten; she wasn't surprised.

Guy Bernabi and Troy were close friends as boys,
When they were together, there was lots of noise,
Their childish minds with curiosity were bent
Keeping their mothers in wonderment.

Guy liked to tease, I am told,
For when Odessa was not very old
He filled her small, red wagon with dirt,
Bringing tears to her eyes, causing her hurt.

When he was older, he stood at the fence between their house and
ours,
Looking for Odessa, employing his visual powers,
Then when he saw her, instead of using her name,
He'd call her "Spring Chicken,"
Leaving her with embarrassment and shame.

Our neighbors, whose last name was Rich,
Provided ways our lives to enrich,
Since there were too many to review,
I'll relate only a few.

Noel, their oldest sibling and only son,
By his sisters was kept on the run,
He had some fascinating insights
As he observed them in their daily plights;

With talks of cooking, appearance, and dresses,
Household chores and styling of tresses;
But he survived, as he'd learned to do,
And was proud of them as each year they grew.

In '36, Zota, after losing the "Peach Queen" election,
Became First Attendant to Bessie Dempsey;
Even though we'd saved coupons for her,
As she was our preferential selection.

She taught a vacation Bible school class that I attended,
And was an excellent teacher—well prepared,
After class, I expressed my thanks to her
To let her know how much I cared.

Mabel Vera, Troy's age, was an attractive girl,
Who could send a fellow's heart into a whirl;
Occasionally, she asked if she could ride with us to school,
And we were happy to accommodate her as a general rule.

A few years after finishing school, she married,
And everything good was going her way;
Later, she gave birth to a darling daughter
Who filled their lives with happiness every day.

Then one day her husband received word that he was needed
To help fight a war for our country's freedom;
So he reported on time to the designated place,
Not wanting to ignore the command, for that would be a disgrace.

Then, some months after being drafted,
He made a decision that seemed thoughtlessly crafted;
He decided not to return to his daughter and wife,
Leaving her with many questions, sorrows, and strife.

Alberta and Dola, approximately the same age,
Enjoyed play-acting;
With empty Rawleigh boxes they set up a pulpit and stage,
Pretending to have church.

Dola must have been the preacher,
But how do I know?
If they took an offering, I can't relate,
But they realized that no service is authentic
Without passing an offering plate.

36

After the meeting ended and the benediction was rendered,
They proceeded to their next activity,
Welcoming any interested kindred.

Because Alberta was easygoing in her own way,
It was a delight to be with her day after day;
Then before they realized, time had passed too fast,
And they became adolescents reaching toward adulthood at last.

Claribel, a year older than me,
Was a very dear friend and neighbor;
She and I found many reasons to spend time together;
Playing hopscotch, jacks, and doing somersaults in suitable weather.

Sometimes we walked from church to our homes,
An act that afforded exercise and pleasure;
Chatting about all kinds of topics,
School, teachers, and times of leisure.

She graduated from the eighth grade ahead of me,
And was now in high school,
Our visits were farther apart;
But we remained friends, and stayed close in heart.

Years later, I heard she married a sergeant,
And had moved to Alexandria, Virginia;
But nothing can erase the memories that were made
In those childhood years;
They are symbols of a time that can never fade.

No other people on Earth anywhere
With our dear relatives could ever compare;
One time when Mother and Dad were ill,
They, with kindness, the gap did fill.

Grandma Van Nattan, along with aunts Rachel and Ruth,
Took the three girls under her roof,
To feed, clothe, shelter, and love,
Our angels were they, sent from God above.

One day when Dola and I were in bed,
Supposedly napping, but playing instead,
Having no worries, no fears, nor cares,
Suddenly we heard someone on the stairs.

Sheepishly peeping from under the cover,
We saw Aunt Ruth, who just seemed to hover
Near our bed; we both grew weak,
We both wondered why for us she did seek.

She drew very near to where we lay,
And I've tried to forget what she did say,
But with her strong, right hand, and that look in her eyes,
We got our due spanking; 'twas no surprise.

Uncle Ezra and Aunt Ollie
Took Troy to live with them;
Many deeds of love they showered on him;
To be of help, his boyish heart yearned,
He washed and dried the dishes in return.

To keep Norman, Uncle Oliver didn't mind,
But Aunt Lizzie was a housekeeper
Of the immaculate kind;
Norman tested her patience, how could she keep mum
When under the chairs he had stuck chewing gum?

Aunt Nora and Uncle Fred, as well as their daughters,
Were thrilled to keep nine-month-old Everett;
They smiled when they heard his baby prattle,
As excitedly, he'd shake his rattle;
Too soon, they relinquished their guardianship
With tears in their eyes, and a quiver on their lips.

Grandma Van Nattan had a special touch
With doing handwork, making quilts and such,
Each of us from several patterns did select
A choice for a quilt which she didn't reject.

After school one day to her house I went,
For I was told that for me she had sent;
She looked at me with no hint of derision
Asking, "Which quilt would you like?
Give me your decision."

As I looked at each offered design,
Considering which pattern should be mine,
My childish heart beat with a rapid whirl,
I said, "I want the Sunbonnet Girl."

Though time has faded that quilt's bonnet,
And there are ragged edges and frays upon it,
That coverlet stitched with tender care,
Stands proof of the love Grandma gave me there.

Grandma grew plants from tiny seeds,
Later, Troy helped her to pull weeds;
Then people came from miles to find
Those plants of the most nutritious kind.

One item from her garden tasted better than it looked,
But we had a mom from the South who knew how to cook,
Because okra, with its slick, slimy texture,
Tasted better fried, than boiled or stewed,
And we tried to be appreciative and not rude.

After slicing the okra thin and not thick,
It was soaked in a well-beaten egg
(To remove its slimy texture, that was the trick);
Then after coating it with cornmeal,
It was fried in butter until crispy, golden brown,

Yielding a nutritious side dish, one of the best to be found.

A successful hunter, Uncle Ezra by name
Unselfishly shared with us his game,
Being generous at heart, he carried out his habit
Of keeping us supplied with rabbit.

Usually Mother the animal would fry,
One time, however, she decided to try
Something different—a stew or hash,
As a result of her efforts, my spirit crashed.

I was ravenously hungry, as a general rule,
Whenever I came home from school,
So to the refrigerator I'd dash,
And 'twas on such a day, I spied the hash.

How much I ate is of no consequence,
I only know that I became tense,
For soon I took note,
That a jagged bone was caught in my throat.

As Dad wasn't home, I called a cab,
While feeling the bone's awful stab.
I climbed a flight of stairs, near a grocery store,
To a doctor's office where I'd never been before.

Speaking to me with an assuring tone,
He took a surgical instrument and probed for the bone,
Then turning, the doctor said,
"I'm going downstairs to buy some bread."

Soon I began the bread to eat
(Not caring whether it was white or wheat),
I was embarrassed with my condition,
Still, the bone didn't change its position.

So the doctor told Mother and Dad
That no other alternative they had,
But to go to St. Louis, to a hospital first-rate,
Where a specialized surgeon could operate.

I went home while they made a decision
About our means of transportation;
Uncle Ezra (God bless him!), volunteered his car,
As ours wasn't reliable for driving that far.

My friend, Lester Finger, brought a bouquet,
Knocked at the door, and ran away,
Because he was shy, as he's been at times since,
But I was touched by his benevolence.

As I was distraught,
And my nerves were taxed,
The doc gave me something to help me relax;
It was so effective that it put me to sleep,
I was out all night without hearing a peep.

When morning came, I wasn't aware
That previously, in my throat, a bone had been there;
"A coincidence," some say, "a thing most rare,"
But I believe that God had answered prayer.

After Aunt Alma married Uncle Ivan, her beau,
They moved to a farm in Sorento;
She always wanted to marry (with this condition)
That the man be a farmer;
So when her wish was granted, she had no contrition.

When Dola and I were in college, we contacted her,
Asking if we could come for a weekend stay
And also bring three of our friends,
Kay Vaught, Arnold Schmidt, and Dwight Horton;

Then we waited to hear what she would say.

Of course, Aunt Alma, with her hospitable disposition,
Replied with a "yes" as her decision;
So later, all of us appeared at their door,
And she must have been glad that there were no more.

As their children were still living at home,
There was a full house;
Joel Edwin (about thirteen), Evelyn (twelve),
And Norris Lee (perhaps ten);
In determining what would interest them,
We hardly knew where to begin.

Arnold and Uncle Ivan had a lot in common
As both had lived on farms all their lives,
And Dwight enjoyed the rural outdoors,
Which was a pleasant change from that in the dorms.

After attending church on Sunday,
We returned with huge appetites, craving food,
But we didn't manifest our desire too overtly,
For we didn't want to appear rude.

Not long afterward, we gathered at a long table,
Laden with more food than we ever desired,
With homemade rolls, fried chicken, and much more,
Our expert cook, Aunt Alma, must have been tired.

Reluctantly, we returned to our college rooms,
Refreshed in bodies; grateful to have spent
A few hours forgetting about book and assignment,
While remembering a memorable weekend
That hadn't cost us a cent.

Mary Jane is a cousin of whom I have fond remembrance,
When I recall times of her appearance;

As she grew up with no siblings with whom to play,
She enjoyed coming to our house for an occasional stay.

June and July of '36 were packed with times to be together,
While giving no heed to the summer's hot weather;
She came to our house where she stayed for ten days,
And with all our activities she must have been amazed.

On one day I styled her hair;
I'm sure it didn't look professional, but she didn't care;
Then on Sunday, after Sunday school and church,
We went to Bronson's for a dinner that was delicious,
And we were even excused from washing dishes.

When Dad finally had to take her home,
I went to her house for three days,
Spending that Independence weekend together
In a variety of enjoyable ways.

We took our suppers to the Durley campground,
And drove to the spring for a wiener roast;
That weekend visit, so carefully planned,
Proved that her parents were thoughtful hosts.

On one Veterans' Day
(Which was then called "Armistice"),
Several relatives met at our house for dinner,
Which I didn't eat, as my throat was still sore
From a tonsillectomy I'd had a few days before.

So Grandpa and Grandma Coates, Uncle Graham,
Aunt Sarah, and Mary Jane
Enjoyed the meal which they heartily consumed,
While I listened to their conversations from another room.

Mary Jane was employed for thirty-nine years
By the Free Methodist Church;
She was secretary and office manager
For the radio program *The Light & Life Hour,*

Where listeners received inspirational power;

She also worked for the "Department of Evangelism
And Church Growth,"
Giving assistance where it was needed the most.

Happily, her retirement gift was a "Roots III
Genealogy Computer Program"
That she has utilized so well
With her *Coates' Genealogy* book;
It's been a greater blessing
Than any of her descendants can tell;
So for taking us down Memory Lane,
We say, "Thank you, Mary Jane."

Uncle Harry, Mom's youngest brother, and Troy
Were born on the same month and day
(Just an interesting tidbit I'll say);
Both share similar personality traits,
And both chose lovely women to be their mates.

For four years Harry served in World War II,
Never complaining about any task he was asked to do;
He showed his pride and took his stand
To keep our country a safe and peaceful land.

Aunt Lillie became his wife when he was twenty-five;
They were married for more than fifty-four years,
Five decades filled with blessings and some tears.

As a barber, he was as qualified as one ever could find,
Master of the art of cutting hair of all kind;
For forty-five years he pursued this vocation,
And owned his own shop; Vandalia was the location.

Aunt Lillie was a long-term employee
At the Farmers' and Merchants' Bank;

She held every position at one time or another,
So she was knowledgeable about finances,
And with other employees held a high rank.

Uncle Harry had a hobby he thoroughly enjoyed,
Woodworking was the craft he employed;
Skillfully producing many a creation,
This avocation brought much-needed relaxation.

From his woodworking shop in the basement,
Came a defining odor, a sawdust scent;
It was a joy to view the finished product,
Custom-made for his home or church;
And to find any more eloquently designed,
Would be an arduous search.

Giving willingly to their church of their money and time,
Calculating every dollar and dime;
And having no children of their own,
Their estate was donated to a large degree
To the Free Methodist ministry

They began the Free Methodist Foundation,
That helped with people's financial planning;
With the expertise of those acquainted with IRS restrictions,
And with some well-informed scholars,
They were spared many tax dollars.

Many gift annuities were given to Greenville College,
Including real estate and stocks by name,
While reducing or eliminating thousands of dollars
Of taxes from capital gain.

After retiring, they moved to a country home on a lake,
It was a peaceful and beautiful spot
Where we loved to go,
For family get-togethers, and to play games

On the grassy lawn;
On those occasions we had so much fun.

Then later, they moved back to their modest house
Where first they began their married life,
Knowing that true happiness doesn't depend
Upon the wealth of a husband or wife.

As both had been raised in homes
Where frugal living was a norm,
They had learned that "doing without" was no harm;
So at a time when they could afford
A more luxurious house, or a more expensive car,
They chose to minimize their desires,
Simplifying their lifestyle even more.

Since Uncle Harry's death in 1987,
His excellent financial stewardship
(Along with his wife's),
Continues to reap its reward;
With assets that go to a variety of ministries,
All donated with thanks to the Lord.

Five days after giving Greenville College
$20,000 for the annual fund,
Aunt Lillie went to meet God;
Knowing that she had heeded Christ's admonition:
"Lay up for yourselves treasures in heaven";
And now, she is rejoicing in that position.

Her will specified over $43,000
For a full-size, 1,200-pound bronze sculpture,
To be placed in Ganton Circle,
At the main entrance to the college campus.

The sculpture, appropriately named
"Divine Servant," by artist Max Greiner,
Shows Jesus washing Peter's feet;
Perhaps, as students, alumni, and friends meet,

And gaze, with awe, on the disciple's face,
This will be a reminder of our Lord's humility and grace.

Grandpa (Harold Oliver) Coates lived an interesting life;
He became a young widower after he lost his first wife,
Eva Van Marter, we never knew,
For she died when our mother was only two;
So Grandpa was left with son Herbert, four,
And daughter Edith, who surely missed her mother even more.

After five years, he married Martha Jane Puckett,
Known as "Mattie," from Kentucky;
They parented four children—a daughter and three sons;
With six as the total, she was always on the run.

She was congenial, the partner Grandpa needed,
His requests most often were heeded;
They were married for sixty-two years;
Their laughs far outnumbered their tears.

He led churches in Kentucky and Tennessee
For twenty-seven years;
Ministering to those who had doubts and fears;
He loved people from the humblest to the elite,
A stranger he never seemed to meet.

While in Kentucky, many churches he built;
For being idle, he bore no guilt,
One of these churches, Mt. Beulah, still stands,
A symbol of an industrious man.

When he was about sixty-five,
He transferred to the Central Illinois Conference;
Where he took the status of "superannuated,"
And made his residence in Greenville;

The home of Greenville College,
Where many of his relatives have been educated.

He enjoyed farming, and even owned a cow;
And as I look back, I laugh even now,
For when the "time change" came, such as Daylight Savings,
He refused to change his clock, whatever the ravings.

The reason, he insisted, is that "A cow can't relate
To whether the sun is an hour early or late;"
By the tone of his voice, and the look on his face,
We knew his assertion was true and could not be erased.

When Dad decided our barn should be built,
Grandpa's help was sought without any guilt;
So he stayed with us until the job was done,
Listening to his anecdotes always added to our fun.

At the first Coates' reunion in '38,
At least thirty-five relatives met (Illinois was the state);
We had eaten dinner and were out in the yard,
When suddenly, Grandma and Grandpa were caught off guard.

They were sitting in a swing, under a tree,
When we heard a loud noise and looked to see
That the rope had broken; they were to be found
Laughing hilariously as they fell to the ground.

I recall a conversation that wasn't planned, I surmise,
When he made a statement that took me by surprise;
With that trademark of his (those smiling eyes),
He related his reasons for good health;
Incidentally, none pertained to any accumulated wealth;
Instead, he was disciplined in matters of rest and diet,
And to good religion he gave due credit.

Then, I was totally mystified, as I sat by his side,
And heard him proudly proclaim,

"I've never taken as much as an aspirin";
And I simply responded with a grin.

Grandpa built their house when he was eighty-four,
(What a man!)
Using native lumber, which he sawed by hand;
Knowing that when climbing on it,
It wouldn't break.

His plan was this: After two hours' work,
He would go into the house and rest;
Then he'd return to his job, for two more hours at best;
His strength he knew how to gauge,
Appropriately, he should be called a sage.

Grandpa, the last of fourteen children,
Had a heritage that gladdened his heart;
His family's ministerial succession
Played an important part;

Not only was his father a minister,
But also a son, two brothers, grandsons, and others;
All served as pastors in the Free Methodist Church;
A study of their lives makes an interesting search.

Grandpa died at age ninety-two;
Attending his funeral were more than a few;
Nineteen ministers were there, with their tributes to pay
To this godly man, who served others day after day.

As a young man, Uncle Herbert, Mom's blood brother,
Moved from Kentucky to Illinois,
To live with W. T. Graham, a minister;
Graham's salary was minimal, I'd say,
So he sold Rawleigh Products to earn extra pay.

As Uncle Herbert needed a job,

He became a salesman too,
Working for the same company;
Gradually, their friendship grew.

Probably by the minister's greeting,
Herbert decided to attend a camp meeting;
That night he was the only one converted,
Which caused some cruel words to be blurted.

Mrs. Lawson, the superintendent's wife,
Voiced her disappointment to her husband saying,
"Well, this has been a water haul";
Hoping it went only to his ears.
But Uncle Herbert heard what she said,
And perhaps felt like shedding tears.

However, as Uncle Herbert was blessed with a strong will,
He moved forward, his calling to fulfill;
He became a minister, comforting others through their tears,
And held that position for fifty-seven years.

Uncle Herbert married Aunt Fadra in 1914,
In a double ceremony with the Lockhards;
Officiating was Reverend Lawson,
The same man in that camp meeting so memorable.

Uncle Herbert and Aunt Fadra parented seven children,
Four girls and three boys,
Our cousins, who have brought us incredible joys.

Merlin and his wife Evelyn were gracious hosts;
(I personally know)
For my family had breakfast with them
While in Canada for the '67 Expo.

Norma, who personified finesse,
Married John Schien,
Who exemplified this quality just as much, not less.

Lorene and her husband, Wayne Groves,

Willingly drove their car
Over Greenville's vales and hills,
Delivering food for Meals on Wheels.

Roberta expanded the family's ministerial clan,
By marrying Lindh Young—dedicated clergyman.

Fadra, called Phoebe, was in Greenville College
While I was there;
She performed an act that I saw and must share;
After she called quits to a relationship with a boy,
She burned all his love letters;
And while watching the letter embers glow,
Sang "Praise God from whom all blessings flow."

Herb remembers some tactics Everett employed
When they were college roommates,
A time they both enjoyed.

Before leaving the room, Everett removed
The money from his pockets,
Leaving it on the table or bed;
When Herb asked him why,
Everett, being frugal, prudently said,
"If I don't take it, I won't spend it."

Robert, the youngest of Herbert Coates's clan,
Was several years younger than me;
But I remember him at a Coates reunion
(With a camera in hand),
Hoping to capture an interesting situation of some relation.

He is an excellent photographer, now as then,
With photos of friends, as well as kith and kin;
Some of these can be seen in the foyer
Of the church in Florida where he attends.

Our step-grandpa, John Van Nattan, was a man highly esteemed;
After his first wife died, life lost much of its luster, it seemed;
So he contacted a pastor friend, Reverend Mayhew,
Asking if he knew any widow who would "grace the parsonage."

Ella Sanders was the woman suggested,
For her godly life he never questioned,
So after a short time, a courtship began,
And marriage soon became their plan.

Ella took a train to Pana for the wedding fest,
Accompanied by Uncle Graham, our current houseguest;
While Grandpa came from Taylorville,
Eager his part of the ceremony to fulfill.

After pledges of love for the rest of their lives,
Reverend Griggs, the pastor from Pana,
Pronounced them "husband and wife."

Grandma married John when she was fifty-four;
So for several years her energies were employed
Serving the people in Grandpa's congregations,
A privilege she thoroughly enjoyed.

He pastored churches in Taylorville, Pana,
Hillsboro, and Mt. Vernon;
Of all of these towns I am aware,
For on different occasions, I have been there.

Odessa visited his church in Mt. Vernon,
And remembers a song she first heard,
No doubt she could sing it and not miss a word,
(Although this assumption might be absurd):
It was "Blessed Be the Name of the Lord."

She also recalls that he owned a black Ford

With high running boards;
It was probably a Model A, but I can't say;
I know that was a popular car in those days.

Grandma and Grandpa had common backgrounds;
Both were lifelong Free Methodists,
A loyalty that was shared with mutual friends;
And it was in Taylorville that she was born,
On March 23, 1869—day to rejoice, and not mourn.

On a cold Christmas Day our relatives met at their house
In Hillsboro, a town not far away;
I was a child, perhaps only three,
And I was as excited as any child might be,
For I was given a set of dishes, or maybe muffin tins,
And my fun as a cook would soon begin.

After dinner, we met outside for a snapshot;
All stood, except Dola, Dad, and me;
I sat on his lap, with my gift for all to see,
A present from Santa just for me.

Grandma and Grandpa's years together
Passed much too fast;
Then God called him home; his heart just beat its last.

Many friends gathered in the Hillsboro church,
To pay tribute to his life,
And give comfort to his wife,
But Grandma was too ill to attend.
However, she knew in her heart that God's word could be trusted,
And someday, she'd see him again.

Odessa was there and recalls the verse read;
"Mark the perfect man, and behold the upright:
For the end of that man is peace."

The Albert Bronson family members were dear;
I remember that year after year,
Aunt Edith faithfully did bake
For Dad a chocolate birthday cake.

A great Christian was she, a devoted mother,
Who admired our dad, her Christian brother;
I shall always remember her prayerful life,
She was loved by all, and was a faithful wife.

Charles and Troy were together a lot,
As similar interests they sought;
And "Little Edith," as we called her then,
Was a vivacious cousin who exuded vim.

Mildred, I remember, played a flute,
While Charles was a carrier for The Sentinel route,
All of the girls did expertly sew,
And each one artistic ability did show.

They played the piano, and together they sang,
With happy sounds their house always rang,
It was a joy to visit them there,
Where so much excitement pervaded the air.

Virginia and I found many reasons
To visit each other; in all seasons,
We played together, and studied too,
The hours always seemed to be too few.

To school in the wintertime we'd take
A container of milk, where we would make
Ice cream with our own recipe;
Creative cooks—that's what we'd be.

Stirring sugar and extract into milk with ease,
We placed it in the window to let it freeze;
By noon time, when we were ready for lunch,
Our "ice cream" was frozen, ready to munch.

Viola, Marion Shepard's date,
Was in an oratorical contest (of all the state);
While in a spelling contest,
She missed the word "label,"
Thinking that it was spelled the same way as "table."

Ella, the youngest child the Bronsons had,
With wavy hair, resembled her dad;
Lorene, forgive me for mentioning last,
Was valedictorian of her high school class.

In college, Dorothy and I were roommates;
On one cold winter morning, so history states,
She and I awakened to a room full of smoke,
Soon I was aware that it was no joke.

Raising myself, I excitedly said,
"Dorothy! Look! Get out of bed!"
Then sitting up a little higher,
I called, "Quick, the room's on fire!"

Not making a move, she I berated,
"Is she," I wondered, "asphyxiated"?
And then I heard her calmly say,
"Orpha, what's the matter, anyway"?

Moving through the heavy haze,
It appeared to be a bewildering maze,
In my hand I took the old kerosene stove,
And placed it on the fire escape, by Jove!

All of our clothes would have to be cleaned,
'Twould be an expensive job, so it seemed,
But Elva Kinney, "Women's Dean of Goodwill,"
Persuaded Greenville College to pay the bill.

Using hot sudsy water, soap, and a broom,
We cleaned every inch of that dormitory room;
And though we didn't finish 'til half-past five,

We were extremely grateful to be alive.

⁓⚮⁓

Aunt Rachel and Uncle Floyd were parents of two daughters
Doris Jeanne and Nancy Sue;
(Jeanne was seven years older than Sue)
And many times if Aunt Rachel had wallpapering to do,
She left the girls with Grandma, knowing she'd know what to do.

When Sue was quite small,
Grandma would rock her to sleep;
And afterward, Sue would wake up laughing,
Almost never did she weep.

Grandma recorded in her diary
That Jeanne had helped cook supper and wash dishes,
Always willing to do her good deeds,
And sometimes both girls helped Grandma pull weeds.

One day, Aunt Rachel sewed an "umbrella skirt" for Jeanne,
But evidently, for Grandma, too ostentatious it seemed,
For she recorded in her diary, "Oh, the fashion, the fashion!"
She must have thought it unnecessary
In those days, when so much was rationed.

After Jeanne graduated from high school,
She entered nurses' training
In the Jewish hospital in St. Louis,
Graduating with high honors,
Making her friends and relatives glad,
Especially proud were her mother and dad.

Later, she married Robert Hess,
And I'm sure I'm not the first to confess
That he was a dentist given high regard;
And after many years, he retired.

Now, they have more time for shopping,

Which Jeanne always enjoyed, whether home or abroad;
But more importantly,
They can make more frequent visits, many or few,
To dote on those darling great-grandchildren;
(Is it still one, or two?)

In Sue's earlier years,
She enjoyed playing an accordion;
But her dad was often concerned,
For it seemed such a heavy load.
Strapped across her shoulder,
It looked more like a boulder.

She was a beautiful girl,
And had a sweet disposition,
So it was not surprising
That at an early age she became engaged,
And soon married David Boswell;
About his background, not much I can tell.

They were happily married,
And became parents of precious children;
But while still young, some physical problems began,
And although medical assistance was given,
There was nothing that could be done;
For cancer had spread to too many organs,
And her life, at just twenty-nine, came to an end.

This is one of the puzzles of life
That we can never put together;
But we know that nothing can sever
Our love from God and the miracle of his grace;
And so we leave the pieces of the puzzle with Him.

One memory of Aunt Rachel
Is her professional wallpapering skill;

Watching her calculate the number of rolls
For a room was a thrill; after measuring its size,
With a perceptive look in her eyes,
She knew what next she should do.

She cut the panels and placed them on a board,
Aligning them to match the design of the piece before;
Then she turned them over, ready to be pasted;
She was a fast worker, no time was wasted.

Occasionally, my sisters and I helped with pasting,
When Mrs. Campbell, her aide, couldn't come,
Even though she reported as a general rule;
But one day Aunt Rachel pleaded for my help,
And as a result, I missed school.

With the first panel ready, she applied it to the ceiling,
As this was the proper place for beginning;
Then, with a brush, she smoothed the wrinkles out,
That she had knowledge of her trade, there was no doubt.

Sometimes she papered four rooms a day,
Charging $2.50 per room as her pay;
With the job finished, the owners viewed each room's alteration;
And they were pleased with the transformation.

Aunt Rachel's phonograph with the trademark Victrola,
Brought musical pleasure to Odessa and Dola;
Looking through the records a favorite they'd find,
Then a crank at the side of the phonograph they'd wind.

Hearing "Moonlight on the River ..."
Sometimes caused their flesh to quiver;
"Colorado," that was the place
Where the moonlight the river did grace.

Two girls were the daughters of Aunt Nora and Uncle Fred,
Both were blessed with hair that was red;
They also shared the same middle name:
They were called Freda Mae and Ola Mae.

Theirs was a mutual love;
Ola Mae addressed her sibling as "Sister";
They were as close as a hand in a glove.

Aunt Nora was happy doing household chores;
Gardening, as well as cooking, was joyously embraced,
Then when her husband returned from work,
She greeted him with a smile on her face.

As a social correspondent for the local newspaper,
Her column gave readers an inside glimpse
Of the news that (presumably) had taken place,
Or, perhaps, was gleaned from gossiping over the fence.

Uncle Fred, a native of Kentucky, moved to Centralia in 1914;
As a car man for the Illinois Central Railroad, for fifty years,
His mind was always keen.

Ola Mae and I spent many pleasant times
In her playhouse in their backyard,
Climbing on a ladder to a room above,
Then returning to our lower "dining" ward.

Her house was across the railroad track from ours,
And once, when walking home from school
She had to wait for a train that was on a standstill,
And in her reasoning, she had no time to kill.

So unbelievably, with my eyes I saw what was happening,
(Something I would never surmise),
She crawled underneath the train,
And proceeded to her house, feeling somewhat vain.

At another time we indulged in a fascinating myth,
Not knowing whether it originated from kin or kith,
Truly we could have been considered maniacs,
As we went on our mission down the railroad tracks.

We mounted the parallel steel rail,
Convincing ourselves that we could not fail
To reach a strip of wood, the trellis,
Where some important information it would tell us.

Balancing ourselves, we walked quite a distance,
Offering mutual encouragement, as well as assistance,
At times, we would have to jump off and wait
For a train speeding by, as though it were late.

At last, we reached a place we hoped was right;
Kneeling down on our knees, we searched with much might,
Hoping a strand of hair to see,
Which would resemble that of our husband-to-be.

With our fingers we scraped away cinders and dirt,
Unconcerned that we possibly could get hurt,
And I tell you the truth, we uncovered there
A strand of genuine, life-like hair!

We never discussed from what source it came,
Whether from cat or dog, or even a dame;
Content were we to let our imaginations run wild,
Projecting our futures while still a child.

Together we pondered in double measure
The earth's revelation of our buried treasure;
True child-like satisfaction was afforded,
For our efforts, as expected, were rewarded.

At an early age we began singing together,
And sometimes wrote our own songs;
Singing "The First Noel" in a Christmas program
Is a memory that has lingered long.

While we were still teens,
We traveled to Jena, Louisiana
To sing in some church-related meetings;
Arrangements were made by Reverend B. H. Pearson,
With our parents' permission.

Our hosts were parents of our friends,
Boyce and Doris Keyes;
With their gracious hospitality
We surely were pleased.

Then, after a few weeks, we returned
To begin another school year;
Ola Mae, a senior, and I, a junior,
Both eager to pursue our educational career.

One weekend while we were home from college,
Pastor MacDonald asked us to sing in church,
And his introduction still brings smiles,
As he said, "This is still Miss Nimmo and Miss Sanders,"
And we sang (in a rather subdued tone)
"I Won't Have to Cross Jordan Alone."

Odessa & Everett

Everett, Norman & Martha Adams
Orpha in window

1922 Edith, Amos holding Bob
Graham, H. O. & Mattie Coates
Troy, Odessa & unknown

1145 Sanders Ave.

Ella Sanders VanNattan Reunion - 1941

Harold Oliver Coates & Eva VanMarter Philo
blended family - about April, 1890

H O holding Charles Herbert Coates, Eva holding Clara Edith Coates
Lillian Philo standing (center); Fred Philo (far right)

H O & Mattie Coates

The Coates Cousins, 1938

Ella Sanders VanNattan Family
Hillsboro, Illinois, 1926

Amos Sanders Family
Coates Reunion
1938

Albert & Edith Bronson Family, 1944

8th Grade graduates
East Wamac School
May, 1938

Grades 1, 2 & 3
East Wamac School
Sept 29, 1925

Troy Sanders

East Wamac School

The 1930 family car with Rawleigh products case -- the "grip"

Back: Edith, Odessa, Amos
Front: Orpha, Dola, Troy
Not pictured: Norman, Everett

Bronson cousins showing off the family car -- about 1934
L. to R.: Edith, Ella (on running board), Viola (back bumper)
Inside: Lorene, Virginia, Mildred

Headed for camp meeting
in our 1936 Chevrolet

Centralia Free Methodist Church

Men's Bible Study Class
Amos Sanders, teacher

Junior Missionary Class
Dola Sanders, teacher

Friends from Centralia Youth group

C B & Q Railway, Troy on furlough, reading the newspaper

The pen, showing the trough where we "slppped" the pigs

Chicago, Burlington & Quincy Railroad - the C B & Q
Sanders' property approx where trailers are shown
the 17th Street crossing -- old U.S. route 51

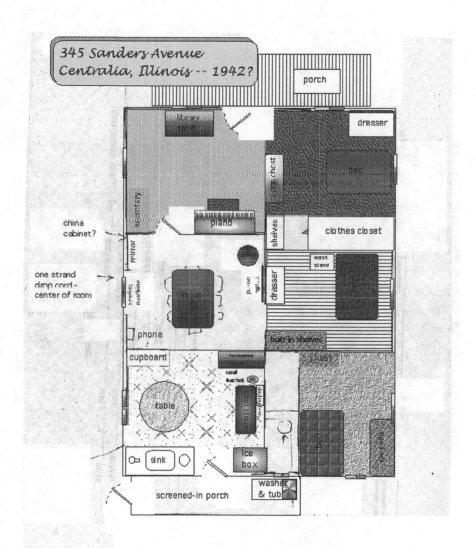

345 Sanders Avenue
Centralia, Illinois -- 1942?

porch

library
room

dresser

bed

china
cabinet?

mirror

piano

shelves

clothes closet

wash
stand

one strand
drop cord -
center of room

dresser

phone

cupboard

coal
bucket

table

table

ice
box

sink

washer
& tub

screened-in porch

The Sanders six siblings
Back, L. to R.: Norman, Troy, Everett
Front, L. to R.: Dola, Orpha, Odessa

The Amos Sanders family
-- shortly after baby Everett arrived - about April, 1929

Amos, holding Everett

Edith

Odessa

Troy

Dola

Orpha

Norman

Amos & Edith Sanders Family
1929 and 1941

Jackson, Michigan, 1958 Reunion
L to R: Odessa, Dela, Orpha, Amos, Edith, Troy, Everett, Norman

Dad's jobs were diverse in nature;
At first, he worked in a shoe repair shop
Above Hart's grocery store;
He was sixteen, possibly seventeen (not any more);
He was a keen observer, eager to learn a trade,
To attempt to mend shoes, he was not afraid.

He learned the art of stitching,
And the quality of leather,
And proved by his work,
That he was mature beyond measure.

But after working at this shop for about five years,
And making only $10 a week of pocket money to keep,
He realized his job he must sever;
So with memories of mending shoes,
And the aroma of fresh leather,
He left in 1920, other employment to seek.

Working in the Centralia coal mine
Was an adventure of a different kind,
Its risks involved seldom surfaced
To the conscious mind;

And although I don't know
The amount of money he made,
With a wife and a small family,
There were always bills to be paid.

Dad loaded cars with coal, using a large fork,
Working with no sunlight, always in the dark;
His thoughts were on his family,
And what lay ahead;
But because he was a Christian,
The future held no dread.

After a few years at the mine, when he was about twenty-six,
He began a job of a far different kind;
It required a positive spirit,
And the ability to communicate well;
He became an associate with
The W.T. Rawleigh Company,
And began to sell.

This proved to be a wise choice indeed,
For he could determine his own
Working hours; and to his family
He could give more heed.

At first, he was a timid walking up to a door;
Knocking lightly, never more;
Smiling while tightly holding his case,
He greeted the customer face-to-face.

Sometimes Odessa rode with Dad on his Rawleigh route,
And when a product was needed
From the back seat of the car,
Wanting to do her part,
She turned around and handed it to him;
A gesture that warmed his heart.

Then, before returning home,
He'd stop at a customer's shop
Where he'd been many times before,
And buy her a pop;
A special treat in those days of yore.

After twenty-five years of service,
He was honored with a diamond pin;
The company respected the loyalty of their men.
That Dad was dependable, they had no doubt,
His record proved his faithfulness
To people on his route.

With this company he worked for about fifty years

And made a good association with his peers.
But one relationship exceeded all others,
And that was with his family;
We could rightfully be called "Rawleigh" fans,
For we grew up with their products,
And claimed kinship with the Rawleigh man.

⁓※⁓

Rawleigh's cinnamon set the tone
For the pumpkin pies baked in our home,
And when pepper was needed to add zip and zest,
Mother used Rawleigh's, for it was the best.

So many times in cold, winter months,
When sore throats plagued us—yes, even the mumps,
Rawleigh's yellow mouthwash, with its soothing foams,
Helped us forget all our aches and groans.

A favorite with customers was the liniment,
While others chose bath oil with peppermint scent;
All of the products were held in high esteem,
They were part of our lives, or so it seemed.

Our cakes and ice cream would have had a real lack,
Without Rawleigh's vanilla or lemon extract,
And with the butterscotch mix, as well as the lemon,
Mother baked pies; she was the queen of all women!

⁓※⁓

About Mom's past history, I will say very little,
For Everett and Jane did such a wonderful job
Of uncovering important information
About her family tree,
And I know that all of my family agree.

She was the most patient person I ever knew,

Standing four feet, ten inches in her shoes;
I never heard her raise her voice to anyone,
And in many ways, she was lots of fun.

She never went beyond the fourth grade in school,
But she lived by the principles of the Golden Rule;
From the *McGuffey Reader* knowledge she obtained,
And her ability to spell was remarkably attained.

The Bible was her favorite book; and if one were to look,
It would come as no surprise
Why its precepts had saturated her mind,
For at the time of her death, she had read it through thirteen times.

If you have a truly good mother,
She is worth more than a precious gem!
She has no fear of winter for her household,
For she has made warm clothes for them.

She is energetic and a hard worker,
And never could be called a shirker;
She is a woman of strength and dignity,
And has no fear of old age;
For she knows most certainly
That immortality cannot be caged.

Her family stand and bless her
And praise her with these words:
> *There are many women in the world;*
> *Some we could easily recall,*
> *But if we were to cast a ballot,*
> *You'd be voted the best of all.*

As a child, our mother had few possessions,
But one which she adored and brought a smile to her face,
Was a doll made of china, a symbol of beauty and grace.

Its hair, also china, was coal black,
With its overall appearance there was little lack;
Because it was so fragile, Mom stored it away,
In a trunk in our clothes closet it safely lay.

Occasionally, she would open the trunk
And remove the doll from its place;
Then, with a wondering look in her eyes,
Perhaps, she wondered what her own mother
Would think and do, if she were still alive;
But she died when Mom was only two.

Easter eggs we colored with a great deal of zest,
Competing to see whose egg looked the best;
The colorful dyes in tin cans were contained,
On one's own egg, we would write our name.

On Easter morning we rose very early,
On that happy day we were never surly;
Taking our brown paper bags outside,
We hunted for eggs, with Dad as our guide.

Surveying the yard, we strained to see
Where the hidden eggs might possibly be;
Near the fence, and 'round the trees we ran,
Talking excitedly as our eyes did scan.

In places nearby and farther away,
We found the eggs, wherever they lay;
Such happy faces as ours must have looked cute,
From the youngest to the oldest, comparing our loot.

However, our parents' aim and intent
Was to teach us what Easter truly meant,
So early in our lives we learned
That by Jesus Christ death was spurned.

Songs of Christ's resurrection power
We sang at the Easter sunrise hour;
Scripture verses retold the story,
How He rose again, from earth to glory.

Each service of the day was a joyful proclamation
That Christ answered death with life's exclamation;
That assurance, still valid, that Christ lives today,
Has taken all fear of death away.

On the Fourth of July, our Independence Day,
Our family gathered at Smith's Grove to play;
Because our Sunday school hosted this special event,
Most of the church families usually went.

Participating in the games was a great deal of fun,
In the three-legged sack it was a challenge to run;
Inside a gunnysack like a rabbit we hopped,
Rushing to a designated line where we stopped.

For the older-versus-younger there was spirited action,
The baseball game was a special attraction;
There were plenty of spectators, who sat quite near,
Encouraging "their team" with appropriate cheer.

If at times, a less active game was desired,
And this was made known by those who inquired,
Sunny Daggett was usually waiting to choose
Someone to challenge him to the game of horseshoes.

Another game I'll mention—how could I forget?

Was the one played with a large ball and net;
Much excitement was always found
As we tried to keep the volleyball from touching the ground.

Long rows of tables were set up on the ground,
Lots of food soon weighed them down;
Those casseroles, salads, and desserts (quite a few)
Were tastefully prepared by a multi-family crew.

In addition to cakes, cookies, and pies,
All the children were given a "cool" surprise;
There were ice cream cones, so many in fact,
That the "children" included Brother and Sister "Mac."

Winter holidays were such happy events;
The long-streaming icicles, draped over the fence,
Became our popsicles, free for the taking,
Leaving mittens wet and hands cold and aching.

Norman and Donald Kent held a special bond,
And of Donald's family, we too were fond;
Seeing their greenhouse was delightful, I admit,
But the activity that was greater fun,
Was ice-skating at holiday time on their pond.

The first winter holiday was near at hand,
And Dad, thinking ahead of our dinner,
Carried out an idea he had in mind
That was of an unusual kind;
He made an offer that was accepted,
Thankful that it was not rejected.

For Rawleigh products some customers traded
A big goose for our Thanksgiving dinner.
But well I remember that Mother picked pinfeathers out
For hours in preparation for that dinner;

So I wonder, "Who really was the winner?"

Thanksgiving was met with pleasant expectation;
At school we flaunted paper turkeys
That we made for decorations;
And always we'd sing our favorite Thanksgiving song:

> *Over the river and through the woods*
> *To Grandfather's house we go,*
> *The horse knows the way to carry the sleigh*
> *Thru the white and drifted snow.*

We really didn't go to Grandfather's house.
Instead, we helped prepare dinner and set the table,
And at intervals, played outdoors,
Building a snowman, or creating an angel
As we lay on the snow.
At long last, our appetites announced, "Go!"

With the goose and all the trimmings,
And those luscious pumpkin pies,
Our feast was ready,
Prepared under our mother's watchful eyes;
Then, by Dad, a thank you to God was prayed,
For all the blessings He daily conveyed.

After the Thanksgiving holiday ended,
We knew Christmas was not far away,
But December was filled with so much activity,
We sometimes wished we could increase our longevity.

Caroling was an event we always enjoyed;
Our dad's chauffeuring was readily employed
As he volunteered to drive the church bus,
Keeping the windshield free of snow gusts.

While sprinkles of snow fell on the ice-packed ground,

Our voices we raised in yuletide songs
With church friends who went along.

As the sounds of carols pierced the air,
Silhouettes of people appeared here and there,
Pushing aside the window curtain,
Affirming what they'd thought might be certain.

Standing there very intent,
Some with shoulders stooped and bodies bent,
They listened quietly as we sang of Christ's birth,
Witnessed by angels here on Earth.

Afterward, we expressed peace and goodwill
To those who were aged, shut-in, or ill;
Hurrying along, in the cold night we lurched,
Shouting "Merry Christmas from the Free Methodist Church!"

Our church gave special emphasis to the Christmas tradition,
With a program highlighted with a yuletide rendition;
Relating the story of Christ's coming to Earth.

With jubilant voices carols we'd sing;
        Joy to the World! The Lord is come;
        Let Earth receive her King.

In one program I was an angel,
Dressed in a long-sleeved robe,
And perhaps out of character (I don't know),
But wearing a new wristwatch, a gift from Troy,
I pushed up my sleeve high enough for it to show.

After the program had ended,
We received a brown paper bag;
Inside was an orange and some Christmas candy;
And even though we received one each year,
It still added to our holiday cheer.

Getting ready for Christmas kept us busy at our house;
For in addition to the activities our church planned,

We made our own decorations by hand.

Mother did much of her work after we went to bed,
For those items that were made on her sewing machine,
Were often secret, not to be seen.

When it was time to put up the tree,
We made sure it would be beautiful for all to see;
Garlands of popcorn that we had strung
Around the Christmas tree were flung;
While circles of red-and-green paper chains
Were draped from the ceiling and windowpanes.

As we had minimal money for buying gifts,
We shopped at the five-and-ten-cent store;
Usually, I bought Dad a handkerchief
(I have no idea how many he had),
But as Kleenex hadn't been invented,
It was a present that made him glad.

Whatever gifts we bought,
We practiced what our parents taught:
"It is more blessed to give than to receive."

One Christmas day which I vividly recall,
Was among the happiest holidays of all.
Dola and I were surprised to see
A bed for our dolls under the tree.

It was custom-built, green it was painted,
To put it mildly, we were elated;
(Guess what we heard?)
Santa's helper was none other
Than Troy, our eldest brother.

Our dolls, with their fur-trimmed coats and caps,
Were cuddled and fondly held on our laps;
Their newly-sewn wardrobes caused quite a sensation,
They were, of course, our mother's creation.

Another Christmas gift I remember
Was a five-year-diary from Mother, when I was ten;
But there were only four lines for each day's entry;
So little I could record about my kith and kin.

However, those written accounts of my life,
And the lives of relatives and friends,
Bring smiles and are refreshing in times of recollection,
And renew my gratitude during retrospection.

One entry I made on a Christmas past was this:
I got a lot of things for Christmas, couldn't name them all.
I think some of my siblings would say:
"When merging those Christmases of yesteryears,
We feel the same way."

A special gift we gave to our parents one Christmas
Required a bit of scheming;
I don't remember whose idea it was,
But we all agreed it would have real meaning.

We called a photographer for a timely appointment,
And then on that day, dressed in our Sunday clothes,
We walked into the studio, ready to pose.

When the photograph was ready, we took it home,
Keeping it a secret, as it was our own.

When Christmas came, Dad opened the carefully wrapped gift
And when viewing the image of his six children,
Tears ran from his eyes;
The photo, as we'd wished, was a great surprise.
(Mother was in the TB sanitarium that year).

Dad was an expert at making peanut brittle.
His famous recipe was no secret riddle.

With caramelized sugar and nuts spread in thin sheets,
The result was delicious, a successful feat.

Sometimes we used the caramelized mixture
For popcorn balls; it gave them a special texture.
It was exhilarating, removing the contents from the pans,
And forming those spherical shapes with our hands.

Making taffy with Dad was also fun,
Boiling corn syrup or brown sugar, the process was begun,
Then pulling on it 'til it turned light,
With candy all over we were quite a sight.

Knowing when it was ready was somewhat tricky,
But we watched each other while our hands got sticky.
Sampling the finished product we were very pleased,
Giving no thought to future dental needs.

Sometimes Grandma made a date roll,
As well as chocolate fudge, that soft, creamy candy;
Or divinity, made with whipped egg whites, sugar, and nuts.
All her confections, so deftly prepared,
Were evident of her love for us,
Showing how much she truly cared.

An incident happened (or so I've been told),
To Troy when he was about five years old.
In the back of the church he fell asleep;
His rest so sound, he didn't make a peep.

When he awakened, he was filled with terror
To find that no one was with him there.
He banged his little fists hard on the door,
Screaming, crying, and banging some more.

When Mom and Dad arrived home at last,

I'm sure that they were completely aghast.
They looked for Troy everywhere,
Finally concluding that he was not there.

So back to the church they drove their car,
It seemed to them unusually far;
You can be sure that they weren't surprised
To find their little boy with tears in his eyes.

One time when Troy was a very small tot,
He was pulling Mom's flowers
When he got caught
Hoping to distract her (so he wouldn't get whipped),
He pointed to the sky; "See the airplane," he quipped.

He pushed Odessa toward the kitchen door,
Teasing her, as he'd often done before
She called for "Papa" (it was safer with two);
Then Troy said to her, "Mama wants you."

Once Troy, his curiosity aroused,
Set fire to a field not far from our house;
He wasn't really naughty, nor was he mean,
But he craved excitement—like a fire truck on the scene.

Troy and Norman were a mischievous pair,
They did some dreadful things that I'd never dare;
Down in the hollowed post on our front porch,
They used a firecracker as a type of torch.

'Round the legs of a sparrow they tied a string,
Then down the post the bird they'd fling,
The firecracker, lit, was dropped on the bird,
Fluffy feathers flew out, as its cries they heard.

One vacation that Dola had
Was in '33 with Mother and Dad;
They traveled to Chicago to the world's fair,
"A Century of Progress" was being held there.

Odessa was unhappy 'cause she couldn't go
To that exhibition—a world's show;
But Dola, at ten, had earned her own way,
By saving the money with her own pay.

Grandma Van Nattan really tried
To console Odessa as she pled and cried,
But the right methods she must have lacked,
For it proved to be a futile act.

A trip to Kentucky, Odessa likes to recall,
(I don't know if it was summer or fall),
Mom and Dad, Uncle Harry, and she
Went to visit our grandparents, the Coates;
And about Grandpa's buggy, she still proudly gloats.

Grandma's meals were always delicious,
In that "Southern" style she learned to cook,
(She didn't need any fancy book)
With those homemade biscuits, and Southern-fried chicken,
They could use their fingers and, afterward, lick 'em.

When it came time to depart, the thought saddened them,
For they didn't know when they'd see each other again,
But they said their goodbyes with tears in their eyes,
And headed their car toward home.

On their way home, before they'd gone very far,
As they were traveling in their own car,
They agreed that because these trips were so few,
Some extra sightseeing they would do.

They decided to visit the park at Mammoth Cave,
As it was always such a rave;
Just thinking about it put excitement in the air,
And before they knew it, they were almost there.

At last, inside the cave they walked,
Listening to the guard as he talked
But when Odessa realized that darkness was every place,
And she could barely see anyone's face,
She was afraid and to the entrance she dashed,
Feeling relieved, yet somewhat abashed.

So the guard unlocked the door,
And she stood outside where she'd been before,
Waiting for the others to return,
And to hear about all they had learned.

About stalactites and stalagmites
She will never know firsthand,
But now she surely understands
That this cave in Kentucky
Is the largest known cave in our land.

Odessa recalls an exciting event
That took place on a hot summer day;
While she was visiting with Aunt Nora and Uncle Fred,
Who lived not far away.

Their old-fashioned telephone rang,
And hurriedly, Uncle Fred answered the phone;
Raising his voice, in an excited tone,
He turned to Odessa to announce,
"You have a big baby boy at your house."

To a nine-year-old this was thrilling news;
She must hurry home; there was no time to lose,

For she couldn't wait to see Norman, her new brother,
And her dad as well, and also her mother.

Fond memories of my eighth-grade graduation I have,
When the graduates of three schools convened,
North and East Wamac, and Washington;
And although it was quite a few years ago,
Sometimes it seems like an event I dreamed.

The boys' chorus from North Wamac School
Sang an appropriate song;
Afterward, A. L. Trout,
(Teacher and coach at the high school) spoke,
And his speech, suitable for our age group,
Was timed just right, not too long.

But the memory that I cherish most,
Was an American Legion essay contest in 1938,
Eleven days before our graduation date.
Offered to the eighth graders of several schools,
Only two winners would be chosen;
A girl and a boy—those were the rules.

After we arrived, the topic was given:
"Why Living in America Is Preferred
To Living in Any Other Country";
Ideas began to flow, and my writing was driven.

The long-anticipated day arrived,
And we were pleased that we had survived
Eight years of education,
And now looked forward to receiving our official certification.

After the boys' chorus had sung,
And before Coach Trout spoke,
The presentation of the award was made,
And my name was announced as the essay's winner;

Naturally, I was pleased, but astonished,
For at writing essays, I was only a beginner.

After the graduation ceremony had ended,
Uncle Ezra asked to see what I'd won.
So I gave him the box, and turned aside,
To converse with my classmates, with whom I had fun.

Soon he returned it, not speaking a word;
And to me, this gesture seemed somewhat absurd;
But later I was happily surprised
For Uncle Ezra, who was as sly as a fox,
Had placed a silver dollar in the box.

Dola, Everett, and I (in different years),
Entered a city-wide spelling bee,
In which nine schools participated,
And each of us was disappointed
When we were eliminated.

Unfortunately, Dola misspelled the word given her,
Even though she'd spent much time in preparation;
But I'm sure she realized
That the many words she'd learned to spell correctly
Were a good foundation for her future education.

When Everett was given a certain word,
He asked for clarification;
"Do you want the singular or plural?"
A question he didn't consider absurd.

Because they weren't permitted to answer his query,
He spelled the word he thought they wanted;
Even though it was spelled correctly,
The number was wrong;
Leaving him feeling somewhat wary.

My problem involved one of hearing;
Although I spelled correctly the word I'd heard,
It was not the word given;
Understandably, my heart was riven.

Shortly thereafter, Aunt Ollie took me to an interesting place;
Not disclosing where we were going,
Perhaps this was more prudent
Than telling me face-to-face.

Later, we entered a doctor's office,
And I noticed he was standing by his chair;
Still, I didn't know why we were there;
I was somewhat surprised
To learn that his specialty
Was in audiology.

After he completed his exam,
We walked out the office door,
And each step I took on that long flight of stairs,
Seemed louder and louder than the one before.

When Mom was told that she had TB,
We were as sad as we could be;
She'd be in a sanitarium for complete bed rest,
Her faith, and ours, was put to a test.

In the fall of '42 I entered Greenville College,
Where Dola was returning,
While Everett was beginning high school,
Eager to pursue his learning.
Norman likewise was in high school, his second year,
And Dad did his best to fill our house with cheer.

We visited Mom as often as permitted,
But visiting hours were very limited;
And while the distance to Ottawa didn't seem far,

We couldn't always rely on our car.

Once we arrived on a Saturday night,
And we must have appeared an interesting sight,
Finding no place to lodge or wash our faces,
We realized we were at the mercy of someone's graces.

So by calling, a Nazarene church was found,
As no Free Methodist churches were around,
The pastor and his wife were most benign,
They invited us to spend the night with them,
A gesture that was so kind.

They served us breakfast as well,
That we were grateful they could tell,
Afterward, we attended their morning church service
That was to begin soon,
As we couldn't see Mom until afternoon.

Mom was smiling when she saw us there,
It appeared that she didn't have a care,
Her spirits were up, not down;
Soon we met her roommate, a lady from our hometown.

From the sparkle in Mom's eyes and the shine on her hair,
We could tell that she was being given good care;
Her routine was so different from that in the past;
For one who had labored diligently for others,
She was now the recipient of all those tasks.

We tried to keep our conversations of an optimistic kind,
Focusing on the path ahead, not on problems behind;
Soon visiting hours came to an end,
And we had to leave Mother, our much-loved friend.

Everett's visitation time was shorter than ours,
It was measured by minutes, not hours;
As he was too young to enter the room, he stood at the door,
Conversing with a Mother whom he adored.

We said our goodbyes and were on our way,
Thankful that we'd had such a pleasant stay,
Committing Mom's health to God's care as He willed,
Believing His purposes were being fulfilled.

After a year, Mom returned home,
With the doctor's insistence that she get extra rest,
Later, the doctor advised a warm and dry climate,
During the winter would be best.

He recommended Arizona, the Grand Canyon State,
Leaving the decision for them to debate;
So this plan was proposed,
With all the implications such a move would impose.

Norman, having completed high school in three years,
Had entered Greenville College with no fears;
Our parents' judgment was that Everett should finish
His senior year at home;
And they did not want him to live alone.

So they asked our friends, Lewis and Dorothy Dillman,
To move into our house,
To be caretakers while they were away,
And then they waited to hear what they would say.

The Dillmans believed this was an acceptable plan,
"We'll do the best we can"
So Mom and Dad were free to move West,
Heeding her doctor's request.

The Dillmans and Everett had a friendly bond,
And of each other they were quite fond,
Except for one time when there was friction,
And Dorothy used some derogatory diction.

Not knowing Lewis liked the center of a lettuce head,
Everett ate that portion instead;

When confronted with his thoughtless action,
He apologized to their satisfaction.

Mom and Dad never did reach Prescott,
For they stayed in a city that they'd given no thought;
After attending the Albuquerque Free Methodist church,
They were persuaded to end their search.

They moved into a trailer,
And Dad found a job as a janitor in school;
There he met pupils of varied cultures and races,
While some were somber,
Others displayed smiles on their faces.

After several months' separation from their family,
Mom and Dad became homesick
For those family members they longed to see;
So they returned to Centralia,
Where they'd lived for twenty-nine years,
In time for Everett's graduation,
And congratulatory cheers.

A fond wish that Mom and Dad made known,
Embraced by each child as his own,
Was a desire for us to have an education in a Christian institution;
Not fully comprehending the costs required
For books, room, board, and tuition.

When the time came for Odessa to enroll,
Being short of funds would take its toll,
Calculating every needed cent in order to learn;
She thought of someone to whom she might turn.

Her kind shorthand teacher encouraged her,
Saying that a local women's club
Would loan her money for tuition;
So she followed thru with this suggestion,

And was able to bring it to fruition.

Another answer to prayer came to pass
Before she registered in any class;
She longed to take voice lessons her first year,
So she turned to a relative familiar with her plight,
And Aunt Ollie helped in a circumstance so tight.

Odessa relinquished her desire to live in a dorm,
When she was offered a room that she could afford;
By agreeing to assist in household chores,
She would receive free room and board.

Singing in the Girls' Glee Club
Was both a privilege and a pleasure,
For she was blessed with a good singing voice,
And this activity gave her cause to rejoice.

She became a close friend to all the members,
And especially esteemed their director, Myrtle Fink,
Whom she fondly remembers;
Myrtle was a cousin of David Kline,
A family as likeable would be hard to find.

In one home where Odessa lived, she was greatly perplexed,
And had ample reason to be,
When her landlady made a decision
With which Odessa didn't agree.

The Glee Club was scheduled for a photo session,
For a few moments on an afternoon,
But her landlady refused to let her go,
Causing her emotions to dive so low.

In another home her bedroom was above an electric shop,
In an enclosed cement porch, with cold that would never stop;
So covers she piled on higher and higher,
Pining for the warmth of a welcoming fire.

At another house she plugged in a miniature heater
For warmth; for the lavatory or bathtub;
Then immediately, all was dark—for it blew a fuse;
Sadly, Odessa knew this was no ruse.

Her landlord yelled with all her might;
And it's surprising the neighbors didn't appear on the site
To call the police and make everything right.

Odessa left college after two years,
For she wanted to repay her bills,
So she moved back to our hometown,
And worked at the Hollywood Candy Company,
A place of renown.

After two years demonstrating her diligence,
She repaid all of her loans,
Sister Odessa moved to Indiana,
To face greater unknowns.

She accepted a secretarial job
At the Free Methodist headquarters in Winona Lake,
And among friends, who seemed eager to please,
She immediately felt at ease.

During that time World War II was taking place,
So her main job as secretary was to correspond
With her church's military personnel,
Assuring them that their church was remembering them,
Knowing that at any moment,
Some could meet danger face-to-face.

While employed at this job,
She met Marian Williamson, her future sister-in-law;
Later, she met Luther, and after a number of dates,
They were married—Odessa was then twenty-eight.

They lived in Michigan, the Great Lakes State,
Where she has lived for many years, up to this date.

God blessed their marriage with two sons and two daughters;
Patty, their first-born,
With her dad in Heaven is now rejoicing,
Where praises they are voicing.

Troy could appropriately be called illustrious,
Because he was so industrious,
He held a variety of jobs
When he began his college education;
As a result, he had minimal time for recreation.

After working in a paint shop during his first semester,
In the second half of the year,
He was a stenotypist for Mr. Harford and George Kline,
Who were raising funds for the college—a job of an altruistic kind.

While in the second year, the registrar's office
Was a place Troy was employed;
His work with those people
He thoroughly enjoyed.

During the summer of his junior year,
He waited tables in the dining hall,
Watching to see when a dish should be refilled;
As a co-worker, he was always "on call."

Many times during the summers,
His work began at an untimely hour,
When Dr. Long gave him dictation at 5:00 am 'til 6:00
Or even later; But never did Troy cower.

For three years, he utilized his shorthand and typing skills,
Working for Dr. Byron Lamson, who was fortunate to find
Such a diligent and proficient secretary,
Who was blessed with a perceptive mind.

As assistant to Dr. Long,
Dr. Lamson's responsibilities were varied;
There was much correspondence, as well as meetings to attend,
But he never seemed too busy to lend time and chat for awhile;
He was every student's friend.

Dr. Lamson's admiration was far-reaching,
Even to Alaska, our forty-ninth state;
And about an incident that took place there,
I'd like to relate.

One day at an art store in Anchorage,
I met an artist who just happened to be there;
Byron Birdsall was his name;
Who has painted his way to fame.

It was my privilege to be photographed with him,
And to read more about his art,
As he traveled with his wife to many countries,
Using God-given talent expressed from his heart.

When I mentioned I had attended G. C.,
We both were surprised—as we had reason to be;
Dr. Lamson was a friend of Birdsall's mom and dad,
And when he was born,
They gave the name "Byron" to their newborn lad.

Troy was fortunate to have earned a scholarship;
With tuition $70, room and board $250 per semester,
Although low compared to today's costly education,
In those days, work offered little remuneration.

Troy formed many friendships during those years,
And as long as mental powers remain,
He can recount some of those memories,
And cite a number of friends by name.

One weekend, he brought Gerald Mikels home with him,
And they, with Odessa and Dola, went some place on a Saturday eve;
But I couldn't express my desire to go, or make known my wishes,
For I had to stay home and wash the dishes.

On Sunday, several of us, along with Sunny Daggett,
Went to the reservoir;
Gerald, in his kindly way, helped me up the spillway,
And assisted Odessa as she climbed down the hills,
(Probably giving her thrills)—as guys know how to do;
I also remember that not only was he funny, but nice-looking too.

Four years of college passed by too fast,
And friends and family gathered with Troy's class at last,
To celebrate with him, as he graduated with high honors;
We knew he was well prepared,
To face the unknown vista ahead,
With confidence, not doubt nor dread.

After finishing high school
With Magna Cum Laude acclaim,
Dola worked for a business in Centralia,
Hollywood Candy Company by name.

This well-known enterprise, where Odessa had toiled,
Moved to Centralia in '38;
The smell of hot peanuts, caramel, and nougat was great;
The wrapped bars were carefully packed in crates,
And shipped by request to companies in other states.

Dola, the accountant, spent much time
Keeping track of every dollar and dime,
Making sure that the companies who had ordered the confection
Had sent the correct payment, with no cause for rejection.

For two years she faithfully reported to work,

She was never known her duties to shirk;
And of her own accord, she helped Troy with school debts,
So he'd have little cause for worry or frets.

Later, she enrolled in G. C.
Proud of the accomplishments of the months past,
And looked forward to becoming a student at last;
She was grateful that she practiced frugality,
And could focus on making college a reality.

As a freshman, she studied the basic courses,
Obtaining knowledge from various sources;
Because she knew the value of preparation,
She prioritized her time, with no hesitation.

She assisted Dr. Woods, the director of the
A cappella choir and the Messiah chorus,
Who also gave lessons to students studying voice.
She was responsible for finding places for the a cappella to sing,
While on their annual tour—usually in the spring,
And also find homes where the members could stay
Overnight, until the following day.

She corresponded with G. C. alumni around the globe,
These letters let alumni know
What was happening at their college,
Nestled in a quiet town,
That offered more than credits, caps, and gowns.

They gave assurance that each grad's career
Was viewed with faith that's optimistic;
That no former student was just a statistic;
That Greenville College wasn't interested
Only in a student's city, birth, and class,
But what was happening in a personal way—not en masse.

In addition to this secretarial position,
She labored in the school's laundry,
Ironing shirts that were starched where wrinkles persisted,

While the number she ironed was mentally listed.

Membership was enjoyed in several clubs,
And as an officer of the student council,
Sometimes she negotiated for classmates—in order to appease,
So with such a full schedule, she had little time for ease.

However, her cousin, Roberta Coates,
Who was married to Lindh Young,
Invited her to a party at their apartment
For games and some fun.

Virgil Kingsley, who was in Dola's class, was also invited;
And he asked her to accompany him,
For he admired her;
This was not just a whim.

After the guests arrived, they chatted
About trivialities and events being planned,
Then turned their attention to the party at hand.

While playing a game, she and Virgil changed partners,
As they'd been asked to do,
Even though there weren't many at the party, only a few.

Later, refreshments were served and thanks were extended,
It was time to leave; the party had ended;
But while Virgil returned with his "switched" mate,
Dola left with Paul Vaught; it was their first date.

Also in school was Kay Vaught, a sister of Paul's,
Who was a friend of Dola;
Often, they met in the halls (or the dorm where they lived),
Or in classes, and the room where students dined,
They shared interests that were on their mind.

During the summer of '42, Dola was invited to Kay's house,
With Kay's parents' permission;

They had met her before and now liked her even more;
They opened their hearts to her, as well as their door.

Knowing of her desire to find a job,
They offered her free room and board,
So hoping to secure work so much needed,
She was overjoyed; and their invitation was heeded.

Soon an office job she found,
Her secretarial skills did abound,
And after working for the day,
In the evenings she helped Dr. Vaught for no pay.

At times, she rode along in his car,
As he made home calls after hours,
Focusing the car's searchlight
On the house numbers at night.

So quickly did that summer fly,
Almost faster than she could blink an eye;
She returned to G. C.—not sure what lay ahead,
For our country was at war,
There was much uncertainty, tinged with dread.

At the beginning of her junior year,
I entered G. C., as her roommate with no fear;
For she was a sister I considered first-rate,
With qualities too many to enumerate.

From the beginning, I took part
In many activities dear to my heart;
Singing in a girls' quartet,
And forming relationships I'll never forget;
Playing speedball was never dull,
But the sport I enjoyed most was basketball.

At the end of my first semester,
I was playing as either a forward or guard,
And had scored twenty-one points for my team,

(This didn't happen in a dream!)
But I experienced severe sudden pain,
Yet I tried not to complain.

I was taken by ambulance later that day,
To a hospital in Vandalia, about twenty miles away,
Because there was no hospital in Greenville at that time;
For those who needed medical assistance,
That seemed a detestable crime.

Because I was under age, my parents' permission
Had to be given for surgery of any kind;
So early the next day, from thirty miles away,
They drove from Centralia;
An appendectomy was performed,
And I logged my first hospital stay.

Before returning to the dorm,
Restrictions were given;
I couldn't return to my room on the third floor,
So I was confined to the infirmary,
Inwardly, I thought, "What a bore!"

Neither could I perform my classwork demands,
Even though semester exams were at hand;
So due to my unlucky fate,
I had to take them at a later date.

After these annoying interruptions,
I returned to my regular regime;
But our country was fighting a war,
And turmoil darkened the scene.

In those first months after Pearl Harbor was attacked,
The enrollment among the men never lacked,
However, at a later date, many men were drafted,
And changes in activities and curriculum were crafted;
The slogan for the student body, as well as the nation,
Appropriately became "For the Duration."

The mixed a cappella tour no longer could be,
Less purchase of nylon was soon a decree;
Gasoline, rubber, and some foods were rationed,
But Americans responded as a committed nation.

When Dola was a junior and needed a business class,
No professor was available, alas;
Neither did she know before she enrolled
No degree in business education was offered,
A fact she wished she'd been told.

So after her junior year, she transferred to the
University of Illinois, in Urbana-Champaign,
And was happy to room with three other students
From G.C., so she didn't complain.

Dola enrolled in the College of Education,
And as she had no other transportation,
She walked a long distance to classes;
But due to her blessings, she felt no aggravation.

The girls took turns cooking,
Trying to be resourceful,
As many ingredients were rationed;
Some were better cooks than others,
Because it was more of their passion.

On Sundays they went to the Free Methodist church
In Champaign, Where Reverend Ellis was the minister;
(I think "Paul" was his name);
He also was a student at U of I;
On Sunday evenings many military personnel
Met for fellowship and refreshments, surely including pie!

As months followed weeks, and weeks followed days,
The girls did their assignments, not looking for praise,
Realizing that with each milestone reached,
They were receiving knowledge

That would qualify them to teach.

When the time for graduation came,
Dola could bask in her fame,
For a plaque in the College of Education,
Lists the "Outstanding Student,"
And "Dola Sanders" is the recorded name.

While Claudine Crozier and Dola earned their bachelor's degrees,
Elva McAllaster and Anna Laughbaum earned their doctorates,
A high academic achievement I'll agree.

Each roommate offered congratulations,
And in return, received felicitations;
Later, as they shared final goodbyes,
Wiping away any tears in their eyes,
They knew special memories would always remain
Of times spent together in Urbana-Champaign.

During the summer of '43, after my freshman year,
I went to Detroit, hoping to find work;
Though 350,000 others had the same intent,
I kept positive and had no fear.

The "Arsenal of Democracy," the city was soon named,
When "manufacturing" became "defense" plants,
Producing war materials, giving them fame.

At the kind invitation of Dr. and Mrs. Vaught,
I was fortunate to stay at their house for naught;
Since Kay had married, they had lots of space,
So Dola and I shared the same sleeping place.

Almost immediately, I found a position,
As the Briggs Plant was in transition;
I was told that this was only the second day
That women had worked there for pay.

We adhered to the same working conditions
That had been assigned to the men,
Which meant standing up for ten hours a day,
Doing arduous work, for much less pay.

My job was inspecting airplane parts,
For the P-38 engine;
A responsible job, for if defects weren't tossed;
It could cause an irreplaceable loss.

Working for forty hours a week, and $50 in pay,
Left little time for leisure, and an even shorter day.
Getting out of bed at 4:00 am to be ready on time for my ride,
Not going out the night before, having to forget my pride.

I dressed in the dark not to bother Dola,
But sometimes this didn't go well,
For one day, at work, I arrived to find
I was wearing different colors of socks,
And to express it with levity, I was a laughingstock!

At the end of the summer, when time to leave,
My co-workers and boss said they would grieve;
They honored me with a going-away gift,
A Parker pen-and-pencil set,
A very kind gesture I'll never forget.

Near the beginning of my sophomore stint,
The faculty held its open house event;
A cordial time for teachers and students to meet,
And for all involved it was quite a treat.

Sam Phoebus asked me to accompany him,
But regretfully, I had to say no,
For the next day was an important debate,
To be chosen for the Elpinice Club,
And for more preparation, there was no "sub."

111

A short time later, Sam came to the girls' dorm,
Carrying a package under his arm;
And after ringing the buzzer,
He left the gift on the steps,
With a note inside, showing his charm.

It was a box of chocolates, and my heart skipped a beat,
As I read the words, "Sweets to the sweet;"
Perhaps a quote from Shakespeare, I don't know,
It was proof his understanding he wanted to show.

The next day came the intercollegiate debate;
And some facts about it I want to relate;
"Should the U.S. form a world police force
Or reorganize the League of Nations?"
I chose the latter, stating positive citations.

After days of frantic reading and memorizing,
Laced with hours of terrible suspense,
Twelve happy girls were admitted to Elpinice;
With the tension mitigated, we experienced release.

I was one of three lucky sophomores,
And Dola was one of six juniors,
While the seniors felt much esteem,
As this was their last year to be on a debate team.

The women of Elpinice, in December '43
Held a party in Miss Kenney's parlor
That filled us with Christmas glee;
A highly entertaining debate was held
On the proposition:
"Resolved, that the belief in Santa Claus
Should be taught to children."
Dotty Bess and Grace Heath showed their consent,
While Ola Mae and Kay Harden
Enumerated their discontent.

Dotty believed children should be taught about old Santa,

Even if they recognized their own daddy,
Stuffed with pillows, and in a bright red suit,
Highlighted with his dimpled smile,
And clad in black boots.

The negative team put their thumbs down on the plan,
Because of psychological, physical,
And emotional reasons;
They wanted this idea banned.

Ola Mae thought it must be confusing to children,
To meet Santa in one store,
And then a block away,
See another one walking out the door.

She was afraid this disillusionment
Would hinder them throughout life,
And perhaps, make them physical wrecks,
Causing all kinds of strife.

This was a difficult debate to judge,
For I hadn't considered Santas as sinners;
Nevertheless, by popular vote,
Ola Mae and Kay were declared winners.

Afterward, some descriptions were given
Of Christmases never forgotten,
Followed by some group yuletide songs;
But we didn't tarry long,
Because term papers were soon due,
And the remaining hours were quite few.

But before we left, Alpha Sisters exchanged gifts;
I was pleased with the one who had drawn my name,
The teacher with such rhetorical fame;
Mrs. Woods gave me a prized gift,
An example of her generous giving,
A book by Dr. E. Stanley Jones titled *Abundant Living*.

I returned to Detroit for the summer of '44,
And I want to give credit to Dr. and Mrs. Vaught
Who were so kind to share with me in countless ways
The blessings God had given to them,
And they gave Him all the praise.

Mrs. Vaught was an excellent cook, blessed with culinary skill,
Her delicious fried chicken satisfied our physical wishes,
And we showed appreciation by washing the dishes.

One day at an amusement park
Mrs. Vaught joined Dola and me;
We came upon a revolving barrel
Where the end we could scarcely see.

Mrs. Vaught, a true sport, tried to walk through,
Though with high heels she was wearing;
After she took only a few steps,
On the bottom she was found,
Where she rolled around and around.

Trying to pull her up, we used all our might,
Three of us laughing, as silly buffoons
Making an interesting sight;
With her arms holding ours,
We walked to the end
With our good-natured friend.

For their church, the Vaughts had high esteem,
And by members they were mutually deemed;
A converted Catholic, Dr. Vaught openly proclaimed
How happy he was to see a person reclaimed.

I remember a specific comparison he once made
Of an "earthly-born" baby (many he had delivered),
To that of a "spiritually-born" child of God;

114

His happiness on seeing one "spiritually-born,"
Was far greater than seeing one "earthly-born."

Those summer months went quickly by
And I returned to Greenville;
I'd soon pass the halfway mark
Yet my major loomed in the dark.

We were immersed with news of war,
And had a dwindling student population,
Only after much deliberation,
I decided to major in biology,
And minor in education-psychology.

Norman and I were partners in chemistry class,
But about composition and properties of substances
And their transformations,
We knew nothing, alas.

The first day in lab
"Make a glass pipette," we were told;
With no idea what that was or where to begin,
Somehow, we muddled through to the end.

No chemistry teacher was available that year,
So Ed Spencer was asked to pick up the rear;
He was one of the best scholars around,
And most of us needed more help, he soon found.

He later became a medical doctor,
Known for his expertise,
And during his many years of practice,
His patients he always did please.

A few years ago Ed left this earth
For his final transition;
And two of his sons, both doctors,

Carry on in his tradition.

⸙

That year in school was influenced
By a new resolve of my mind,
I tried to remain positive
In spite of circumstances of another kind;

Instead of lamenting wartime privations,
Such as gasoline coupons and books of rations,
They became symbols of a shared commitment,
That brought healing and less resentment.

Some of the popular music of those war years
Boosted the students' morale;
I laugh as I think of one song even now.
'Twas a silly piece, "Mairzy Doats,"
Enjoyed by both guys and gals.

Two of the numbers that tugged at our heartstrings
Were reminders of what separation means;
"I'll Walk Alone" and "I'll Be Seeing You"
By Dinah Shore and Bing Crosby;
Who entertained soldiers, many still in their teens.

Another song based on a real-life close call,
Told of a pilot on an African mission,
Who was "Comin' in on a Wing and a Prayer";
And in our weak imaginations his anxiety we could share.

One of the experiences of that year
That brings smiles as well as a tear,
Was singing in a girls' quartet,
And those occasions I can never forget.

Each member from a different class, voices all pure,
Dona Cooper, a freshman; Vera Lindsey, a sophomore,
Anna Lee Tracy, a senior; and I a junior.

Sometimes we sang on Sunday at 11:00 am;
Not a gospel song or a favorite hymn,
But a "Prelude"—a call to worship;
The signal the service was about to begin.

The words were fitting, and conversations ceased,
As the church was infused with a sense of peace.

> *Lord, I have shut the door,*
> *Speak now the Word*
> *Which in the din and throng*
> *Could not be heard;*

> *Hushed is my inner heart,*
> *Whisper Thy will,*
> *While I have come apart,*
> *While all is still.*

Some Sundays, with Professor Holtwick
Acting as both teacher and friend,
Driving us in his own car,
Other churches we'd attend.

Usually, he would give a short update
About the college, and its need for funds;
Hoping their hearts would be inclined
To place some money in the offering plate,
Any size donation would be just fine.

Often it would be quite late
By the time we returned to Greenville;
So we paced the next day with a slower gait.

Besides singing in a quartet and the a cappella,
As well as the Messiah chorus,
I assisted Professor Woods in a music endeavor
Which from my memory I can never sever.

The Free Methodist church a new hymnal did need,
Several books of hymns I was asked to read,
Tabulating the number of times they were listed,
To find those most often acclaimed
By the frequency of which they were named.

It was fascinating to note that the hymns I recall
As being the most widely praised,
Were those by Charles Wesley;
The greatness of God they raised.

It is incredible that Wesley wrote over 6,500 hymns
That are sung around the world;
And one of the favorites of all, which Dad loved to sing,
Was "Love Divine, All Loves Excelling,"
Of the glory of God he was always telling.

> *Changed from glory into glory,*
> *'Til in Heav'n we take our place,*
> *Till we cast our crowns before Thee,*
> *Lost in wonder, love, and praise.*

Also during my junior year,
I edited The Vista, our yearbook;
And having worked for four years on my high school newspaper
(The Sphinx, which took national recognition),
With writing, editing, and layout,
I could proceed without a doubt.

Working with me was an excellent team;
Barbara Marston, the associate editor,
I held in high esteem;
While Elzie Pepple, the business manager,
Sold advertising and kept track of all payments received;
He performed his job so aptly,
That Don Mohnkern, his assistant,
Was always relieved.

My responsibility was to direct the staff,
Create a pattern, and work on their behalf;
I'd list the content of each page in the book,
Crucial requirements for a coherent look.

Because our country was still at war,
Many supplies were not in store;
Professor Cunningham, our photographer, was affected,
When often his needs were neglected.

One day, while in front of a group,
He snapped his camera,
And the flashbulb made a loud pop
(Causing a little scare);
So all phototaking had to stop,
But fortunately, he found a spare.

A shortage of supplies and quality
Applied to the printing as well;
I was disappointed to learn
The yearbook paper I knew was the best
Was not available, so this ended my quest.

At the end of the year, the books were distributed
'Midst gaiety and jubilant cheer;
Classmates requested friends' autographs,
While other notes, more anecdotal,
Brought occasional laughs.

I was pleased that the yearbook
Was received so well;
It was a treasure highly prized
In all alumni eyes,
And we were glad we did our part
To instill lasting memories in many a heart.

On April 12, 1945, during my junior year,
The members of our school's debate clubs were honored
To attend a banquet in Hillsboro;
We hadn't traveled very far,
When we heard an important broadcast
On the radio of our car.

Incredibly, the broadcast declared
That President Franklin Roosevelt was dead;
His death occurred at a favorite spot,
A place called "The Little White House,"
A mineral spring that he had bought.

He had purchased the health spa years before,
And literally had opened its door,
He transformed it into a treatment center
For patients suffering with polio.

He was our country's longest-serving president,
And had led us through the Great Depression,
As well as World War II;
So in my heart, I felt the appropriate thing to do,
Whether a Republican or a Democrat,
Was to be grateful for his loyalty,
While we recalled his Fireside Chats.

A high spot of my junior year
Was the Junior-Senior Banquet
With its Swiss-setting theme;
Sometimes, it seems like a long-ago dream.

Our class spent many hours
Building a life-sized mountain hut
In the corner of the dining room;
Adorned with trees and pictured views

Of snow-capped mountains
And green-valley hues.

Through a thicket of small trees,
And over a rustic bridge,
With running water below,
Guests walked to the tables,
Where Alpine-costumed waiters and waitresses stood
With faces all aglow.

Minutes later, preceding a delicious meal,
A triple trio of junior girls sang "The Blessing,"
While silently, thanks was offered,
With an equally silent "Amen."

Don Trowbridge, president of the junior class
And toastmaster of the banquet,
Spoke on the theme, "Men to Match My Mountains,"
Concluding with the stirring poem
With that same name,
By Sam Walter Foss, a poet of acclaim.

Later, Sam Phoebus spoke of the seniors' outlook
As a "Vision from the Mountain Top";
And Wesley Smeal paid tribute to the members
Of the two classes,
Who were serving in the armed forces;
Using the topic "These Love Thy Rocks and Rills,
Thy Woods and Templed Hills."

By then a nostalgic feeling
Clutched at the hearts of all,
But particularly at those students who felt alone,
As Professor Woods affectionately sang,
"The Hills of Home."

Following these sincere reflections,
Dr. Long gave a brief address

On the topic, "The Everlasting Hills,"
Listing enduring qualities to be cultivated,
As love, character, friendship,
Spirituality, and ideals;
Then the triple trio sang the song "Mountains,"
And the film Heidi was shown.

After a delightful evening, students, guests,
And faculty departed,
Going their various ways;
While vivid memories of that special evening
Lasted for many days.

That night, April 27, 1945,
Was significant in other ways;
Not only was it my first date with Don,
But it was Mom and Dad's twenty-eighth wedding anniversary,
Both memorable days.

During my junior and senior years,
The a cappella choir consented to an all-girls' slate,
At first, the tour traveled through Illinois and Indiana,
But in '46 it added to the list Michigan state.

It was both a privilege and an honor
To sing with that group,
As we used our spring vacation,
Traveling by bus, not by car,
Chatting, when awake, or sleeping,
If we'd trekked very far.

We presented a variety of numbers, all sung by rote;
Some "Reformation" hymns of the chorale type,
As well as some spirituals,
Adding a plaintive, highly rhythmical note,
As several folksongs do,
Such as "My God and I"; a favorite of mine.

And the choir ended the programs
With their benediction number,
"The Lord Bless You and Keep You ..."

Traveling with us was Lois Woods,
The director's wife,
Who was also my teacher and a personal friend;
She accompanied the a cappella
On almost thirty strenuous tours,
Showing her loyalty to the end.

Not only was she my freshman rhetoric teacher,
But a Sunday school teacher as well,
She was courteous, gracious, and Christ like,
That she was mindful of our feelings we could tell.

She stated in a conference
Of Christian English teachers,
"Self-expression is not the only goal,
But a self that is fine to express."

Teaching sentences and paragraphs
Was not her foremost goal,
But developing a godly character,
Resulting in wholeness in body and soul.

She and Dr. Woods were the sponsors
Of my senior class,
And held a record that would be difficult
For anyone to fulfill,
For they were chosen class sponsors more years,
Than any other faculty couple in Greenville.

During the summer of '45,
I could be found working
At Walgreen's in my hometown;
Not only was I a cashier, but a waitress,
And sometimes a cook;

It seems that I did almost everything in the book.

One day a man entered the restaurant,
And after enjoying his meal,
He stopped by the cash register,
To pay his bill;
He said to me, "Come outside a minute,
I have something I want you to see."

Once most of the crowd had left,
I walked a few steps to the street,
And peered in the window of his car,
And lying on the seat,
Half awake, and half asleep,
Was a baby alligator, not making a peep.

But the incident I most vividly recall,
Is the most memorable of all;
I was washing dishes (after hours)
On a volunteer basis,
Because the dishwasher had broken;
Our work was proceeding in very slow paces.

When all of a sudden sirens and bells began ringing;
So 'midst soiled dishes, and with suds on our hands,
We hurried outside to survey the scene,
Wondering what all the commotion could mean.

And then we heard the exciting news,
That Emperor Hirohito of Japan
Had surrendered to General MacArthur,
And the Allies were in command.

All traffic stopped, horns were honked,
The crowd let out a roar,
Cheering and dancing in the streets,
Something we'd never seen before;
"V-J Day," August 14, 1945

Was the end of the Second World War.

My senior year in college was to begin that fall;
Thinking back to those high school days,
When I'd wondered if
I could pay for any year at all.

But perhaps this is the time to tell
Of God's intervention (when I was sixteen),
I committed my life to Him,
Asking for His direction in the steps I'd take,
Not to make the wrong choice, proceeding on a whim.

Attending college was my first choice,
But our shortness of money was always the theme;
So I decided to enroll in nurses' training,
An interest more than a fanciful dream.

When I was a senior in high school,
My English teacher informed me
About an essay contest being sponsored
By the Women's Relief Corps
That I'd never heard of before.

She reported a college scholarship
Would be awarded
To any school of the winner's choice
(In the state of Illinois);
So I decided to enter, but feeling somewhat coy.

The topic pertained to Abraham Lincoln's
Domestic and Political Responsibilities,
With two contests—both regional and state,
Preparing at first for the regional date.

I could be found at the Centralia Public Library,
For many hours, on numerous days

Perusing books about the life of Lincoln,
With all the information, I was amazed.

After some time had passed,
I was seated at my typewriter, in my typing class,
When my teacher walked to my seat,
And told me that someone at the door,
With me wanted to meet.

I had never seen this person before,
But she was a representative of the Relief Corps,
And she announced the regional contest I'd won,
My essay could now go to the state.
The true contest had really begun!

So with a ten-day deadline,
Some revisions were made,
And I sent the essay to the specified place,
With a satisfied look on my face.

In the meantime, I pursued another plan, just in case,
At the city hospital—St. Louis the place,
I took my pre-entrance nursing exam
To qualify for nurses' training,
For only a few weeks were remaining
Before college enrollment began.

Soon after, I heard from the hospital,
Saying I was accepted to nurses' school;
Ironically, shortly before going to St. Louis,
I received a call saying I'd placed first
In the state competition;
The scholarship I'd won was valued as a jewel!

Eager to tell Mom the good news,

I scurried across our well-polished floor,
As though I were in a race,
And I almost fell flat on my face.

Later, I pondered: "Did God shut one door to open another?"
Or "Did He open one door to shut another?"
But this I learned: "It is always safe
To trust an unknown future
To a known God."

Academically, the most challenging year was my last,
Nevertheless, the months flew by quite fast;
With Embryology I was completely fascinated,
While Tests and Measurements I didn't care for at all,
But I enrolled in that course
Because it was recommended by Dr. Alvin Quall.

In the last semester Directed Teaching
Was my main course,
And my students, mainly high school sophomores
Who enrolled in biology,
Gave me no reason for remorse.

Dr. Quall was my instructor,
A teacher both knowledgeable and kind,
Who gave much consideration
To the need for proper motivation.

I had complete responsibility
Not only of lesson preparation,
But of devising tests and grading papers,
As well as readying equipment for lab,
Making sure that students' work
Was appropriately tabbed.

Concerning disciplinary problems,
I had none at all
(Which I'm sure must have pleased Dr. Quall);
And for my final grade,
Surprisingly, he gave me an A,
Even though he stated
At the beginning of the course,
That he gave no A's at all.

As vice-president of the senior class,
As well as the student body,
I had few responsibilities;
And I concluded that the titles
Were more symbols of respect,
As every year I was an elected officer;
And on this I like to reflect.

As ours was the first graduating class after the war,
We presented a special program;
Entitled A Song for Tears,
Written by Bernice Vanderhoof, a gal blessed with talent,
And this play was certainly proof.

I was given the responsibility
Of being the general chairman,
Overseeing the production of the tableau and songs,
That showed how God
Cured heartaches and wrongs.

The underlying theme was based upon a song:

Where broken vows in fragments lie,
The toil of wasted years,
Do Thou make whole again, we cry,
And give a song for tears.

My college days came to an end,
And I realized that a new day would soon begin;
With fresh hopes and opportunities,

More joys and sorrows,
All waiting for a new tomorrow.

I was happy to realize that I was a member
Of the Alpha Kappa Sigma Honorary Society,
And had been selected to
"Who's Who Among Students in
American Universities and Colleges."

But the news that gave me most satisfaction,
Was that which I received from Mother
Saying that Dad, without our knowledge,
Had received his G.E.D.
And could now be eligible for college.

Then, after commencement had passed,
With my diploma in hand,
I left my alma mater,
With a prayer that I might lessen strife,
And carry a bit of sunshine into some life,
So someone could say,
"I'm better because she passed my way"

After teaching high school for a year,
Don and I were married with much cheer,
On June 15, 1947, in Decatur, Illinois;
And my greatest joy, that I proudly relate,
Was having my family to participate.

My two sisters, Dola and Odessa, were my attendants
Both beautifully and similarly attired;
While Don's brothers, John and Bob,
Did what for the groom was required.

Dad walked me down the aisle,
In a slow and reverent style,
While seated guests, so many indeed,

Smiled as they watched and waited
For the ceremony to proceed.

Everett accompanied on the church organ,
And a friend of the Trowbridge family,
Warren Tippett, sang favorite nuptial songs:
"I Love You Truly," "Oh Promise Me,"
And my favorite one,

> *O perfect love,*
> *All human thought transcending,*
> *Lowly we kneel in prayer before Thy throne.*

And later, while we were kneeling there,
He solemnly sang "The Lord's Prayer."

Dr. Roland Price, a friend of Don's,
A professor at McKendree College,
Officiated in our double-ring ceremony,
Announcing the beginning
Of what was to be a long matrimony.

While we were still at the church,
A telegram arrived (and we were so surprised)
From Troy and Rosemarie in Germany,
Informing us that their thoughts were with us,
Even though they couldn't be there.

Our wedding trip took us to colorful Colorado,
And our hearts were delighted
With all the beautiful scenery we sighted.

Colorado Springs was our main stay,
So we visited Pike's Peak, not far away,
But within twenty feet from the top
Because of snow so deep, we had to stop.

In Manitou Springs (at the foot of Pike's Peak),
We viewed the Indian cliff dwellings, row upon row;
Presumably built by the Anasazi tribe,

More than seven hundred years ago;

While the Garden of the Gods
With its white and red rocks
Was another intriguing retreat;
Knowing that within this landscape,
The Rocky Mountains and the Great Plains meet.

Those days seemed like a fanciful surprise,
And flew by more quickly than we could surmise;
So reluctantly, we left that mountainous state,
To return to Illinois, whose prairies await.

Don received divinity degrees
From Asbury Seminary, in Kentucky,
And from Garrett Biblical Institute, in Illinois;
While as a high school teacher I was employed,
Earning money to pay our bills and do things
Which we both enjoyed.

Several years later, two lovely daughters blessed our home;
Nancy and Mary, born on the same day,
Exactly four years apart,
Both very dear to our hearts.
Mary, in Alaska, has two lovely girls of her own,
We keep in touch by e-mail and phone;
Nancy in Florida to adventure is prone.

Don pastored Methodist churches for twenty years,
And as an army chaplain counseled soldiers through fears;
Throughout this time, we traveled on land and sea,
And lived for three years in beautiful Germany.

Later, Don worked for both Greenville College
And Campus Crusade for Christ,
Where the rewards were worth far more
Than any required sacrifice.

Don and I were married for thirty-four years,
Laced with adventure, happiness, and tears;
Then, at sixty-two, his life ended too early;
Leukemia and pneumonia—they were so surly.

Dr. Joe Wheeler aptly has stated:

> *Life is short, life is frail, and there is no guarantee of a tomorrow.*
> *All we have is today, this moment,*
> *and the people who come our way.*
> *In the end, our money, things, houses,*
> *and land will be passed on to others.*
> *The only thing that will remain to show that we lived on this earth*
> *will be the impact of our life, acts, and words*
> *on those whose lives intersected with ours.*

For fifteen years I remained single,
(Although I continued to intermingle);
While for fourteen years I was employed
With the Jack Van Impe Ministries,
A position I thoroughly enjoyed.

As a receptionist and proofreader, I was in much demand,
My skills were utilized to the fullest degree,
When I proofread *The Van Impe Prophecy Bible*
Straining my eyes 'til I could barely see.

While there, I met a Canadian board member
Leonard Barnes, in the month of December;
We were married in October of '95,
Then after nine years, sadly, he died,
And still in Michigan I reside.

Dola and Paul were engaged

While she was still in G. C.,
But a date for the wedding couldn't be set,
For Paul had been drafted into the army,
And a time for a furlough they couldn't foresee.

Of the Engineering Corps at Harvard, Paul was a member
Working at Cushing Hospital in Framingham,
Caring for wounded soldiers in World War II;
Too many to be counted, a vast needy crew.

Later, while at Harvard Medical School and on furlough,
He and Dola were married on December 21, 1945,
In Ferndale, Michigan, his hometown;
While he was in uniform,
She wore a beautiful wedding gown.

I was the maid of honor, and Glenn White was best man;
Everett, the only other family member there,
Accompanied on the piano,
And nuptial melodies filled the air.

Reverend Dale Cryderman, a longtime friend,
Performed the beautiful ceremony,
Giving us pause for thought;
After vows were expressed,
With a prayer they were blessed,
And we were introduced to Private and Mrs. Paul Vaught.

Following a reception, they were on their way
To Canada for a honeymoon stay,
But without the right papers,
At the border they were stopped,
So in Michigan they stayed;
They weren't completely dismayed,
For as husband and wife,
They were focused on their future life.

While Paul was in medical school,
Dola was secretary to the president

Of D. C. Heath Publishing Company,
Where she had access to many books,
And was free to browse in all the nooks.

About a year after the war ended,
Medicine's long hours troubled Paul,
So he resigned from medical school,
And teaching in Fowlerville was their new call.

While Paul taught science in grades seven through ten,
Dola taught high school business classes;
But because after-school activities were not to her liking,
She decided to teach elementary school then.

Later, Paul taught at a vocational school,
Where boys were serving for crimes
Ranging from truancy to murder;
Kids with different values but certain desires,
Needing someone to show them how to aspire.

Dola worked toward a Masters in education
With a Michigan state certification;
Later in 1970, she received this degree;
With a focus in reading from Oakland University.

While living in this area,
They were blessed with much joy,
When Robert Kelly arrived on April 4, 1951,
A beautiful, healthy boy.

Teaching boys with emotional problems,
For four years proved quite draining,
So Paul's thoughts turned to dentistry,
To the University of Detroit for training.

Some time went by after he had applied,
And not receiving a word,
Whether he'd been accepted or rejected,

A job in life insurance occurred.

On the day he completed his training,
A letter arrived explaining
He'd been accepted to dental school;
So he attended from 8:00 'til 5:00,
And worked a job from 5:00 'til 1:00;
A plan that was necessary,
For he had a wife and a three-year-old son.

After this grueling schedule,
Graduation finally arrived;
Soon, for patients' dental needs he was caring,
They had all survived!

Then after two or more years had passed,
Paul and Dola learned of a boy, about eight or nine,
Who needed a home;
And they felt theirs would be fine.

Gary was three weeks older than Bob,
And as Bob's adopted brother,
They had many enjoyable times,
While learning to share with each other.

One day, after finishing college,
While riding a friend's English bike,
A traumatic accident happened,
That caused him relentless strife,
Leaving Gary a quadriplegic for the rest of his life.

He has worked part-time,
But finds life can be brittle,
In ways that a normal person knows very little;
But his spirit is strong,
And his trust in God is secure,
Even though at this time, there is no cure.

Both Dola and Paul had illustrious careers,
Teaching and practicing dentistry for many years.
Then at age seventy-one, Paul died,
While memories of his life always abide.

⤙⤛⤜⤝

Troy enlisted in the Army Medical Corps,
After Japanese planes on Pearl Harbor did soar;
His research during those years
Resulted in recognition by his peers.

Some articles were published
In journals—technical and scientific;
Yet, praise he didn't seek.
His college majors—bacteriology and chemistry,
Contributed to his success; they were the key.

For of a Chemical Corps Development Lab
He was deputy commander
At Pine Bluff Arsenal in the state of Arkansas;
This project had a ninety-million-dollar tab.

Two assignments in Europe took him to Germany,
Where his secretary he dated, so attractive was she;
He asked her if she would become his wife,
Her answer ("I will") changed her life.

Later, he went to Headquarters, Third US Army,
An assistant army inspector general was he,
Traveling by plane, as well as by car,
He inspected army posts both near and far.

The Army Commendation Medal
Was an honor he was given,
As well as several decorations
And different kinds of ribbons;
These awards brought satisfaction and joy,
Signifying a job well done

By my wonderful brother, Troy.

Although he was a private in the first of his career,
He retired as a lieutenant colonel after twenty years;
But his greatest achievements, he makes very clear,
Are his wife and four children
Who bless him with cheer.

⁓✵⁓

Norman enlisted in the Maritime Service in '45,
And Mom and Dad prayed daily that he'd be kept alive;
He was commissioned a warrant officer,
While in school at Sheepshead Bay,
But for all his work, he received little pay.

While on assignments in Alameda and San Francisco,
He learned of a possible rotation,
What a situation!
So he and Violet Goodrich, his fiancée, decided to marry;
There was little time for them to tarry.

So in San Francisco, with much trust, and no fears,
And no relatives there to watch and shed tears,
They became husband and wife;
A marriage that's lasted for sixty-five years.

In the fall, Vi returned to G. C.,
Fulfilling a promise made to her dad;
For he wanted his two daughters to earn a degree,
Something none of the Goodrich clan had.

Norman's presupposed rotation,
With ten months on a ship,
Was never carried out;
Instead, his stateside duties were challenging,
Of that there's no doubt.

His work in the Marine Hospital in San Francisco,

Provided opportunities
For his medical knowledge to grow;
He even took care of prisoners injured in the Alcatraz riot!
His job was far from quiet.

After twenty-two months, with his tour completed,
His positive energy was not depleted;
So he returned to G. C., ready to enroll again,
In time for the second semester
Which was about to begin.

After completing college in '49,
His jobs were of a medical kind;
He served as administrator
Of two hospitals in Ottawa—Illinois is the state;
With responsibilities too numerous to relate.

Later in Michigan, his expertise grew,
In Bad Axe, West Branch, and Petoskey too,
As he made many decisions of an administrative kind,
Taxing not only his body, but also his mind.

Now as he ponders those days of yore,
Memories of serving surge o'er and o'er;
For he learned wonderful people are everywhere,
And there's always plenty of love to share.

Many pursuits in college Everett explored,
With music and photography he was never bored;
But his most enduring memory
Of those years in the past,
Was dating Jane and forming
A relationship that would last.

Soon after marriage, he entered the Army Band,
And when the director in command
Inquired, "What do you play?"

He knew exactly what to say.

Asking the director what they needed,
"Oboe" was answered;
So Everett played, and the request was heeded.

To many places they traveled, near and far,
By truck at times, or a military car,
Playing for the Kentucky Derby and other events,
While sleeping at night in army tents.

After the military, he enrolled in Indiana State,
Hoping to take advantage of the G.I. Bill,
For only $135 per month for tuition and all,
His dreams he could fulfill.

After receiving his master's degree,
Dr. Long offered him a position at G. C.,
So back to Greenville they moved once more,
Believing God had opened this door.

Later, they returned to Indiana State,
Working on his doctorate, his teaching could wait;
When his studies were finished, they were overjoyed,
And they returned to G. C. where he was still employed.

During those years, too full to measure,
Their home was blessed with precious treasures,
Two sons arrived to bring joy to their hearts,
David and Greg, four years apart.

Dave's brief life on this earth was a blessing to all;
Courageously, at nineteen, he answered Heaven's call;
But God's daily grace has been on their side,
While Dave's testimony shall ever abide.

Those yesterdays have passed at any rate,

And new challenges we anticipate,
But precious memories never end,
They are revered as a special friend.

Wisdom has been our teacher,
And patience our daily guide,
As we've traveled this journey together
Hand in hand and side by side.

Acknowledgments

I am indebted to the following people and sources:

Aunt Ruth Anderson, who provided information about Dad's early work experiences.

Ella Van Nattan's 1942 diary.

Several issues of *The Papyrus*, which provided information about the activities of Greenville College.

Greenville College Record (January 1958) "Lois W. Woods Memorial Number" for information about Lois Woods.

Much of the information about the finances of Aunt Lillie and Uncle Harry appeared in *The Greenville Record*, (Summer 1999) in an article entitled, "Lillie Coates: A Model of
Planning and Generosity," by Stanley B. Thompson, president of The Free Methodist Foundation.

Journal of the Michigan Dental Association, February 1995 issue, for the article, about Paul Vaught, D.D.S.

The Living Bible Paraphrased, for quotes from Proverbs 31.

Mary Jane Coates, for information from the *Coates Genealogy* book.

Dr. Joe Wheeler for giving me permission to use an excerpt from, "I

141

Can See Him," *Heart to Heart Stories of Friendship* (Carol Stream, IL: Focus on the Family/Tyndale House, 1999, p. 253).

The kind staff of the Outreach and Bookmobile Services of Rochester Hills Public Library.

My brothers and sisters who have been so gracious in allowing me to share their personal experiences, especially my brother, Everett Sanders, for spending many hours sorting through his vast collection of family photos and compiling the photos for this book.

My nephew, Ken Sanders, for using his artistic and technological talents to create the cover for this book.

My daughter, Mary Meade-Olberding, for extensive help in editing and final revisions.

Songs and Poetry:

"Good Morning, Merry Sunshine," written by unknown.

"Lord, I have Shut the Door," written by William M. Runyan, 1923, Renewal 1951, Hope Publishing Co.

"Love Divine, All Loves Excelling," words by Charles Wesley, 1747, and music by John Zundel, 1870.

"Oh Perfect Love," words by Dorothy Gurney, 1883, and music by Joseph Barnby, 1890.

"Transformed," words by F. G. Burroughs and music by Bentley D. Ackley, 1920.